CHEESECAKES

Maggie Black

Cheesecakes

Ward Lock Limited · London

© Ward Lock Limited 1984

First published in Great Britain in 1984
by Ward Lock Limited, 82 Gower Street,
London WC1E 6EQ, a Pentos Company.

Text filmset in 10/11 pt Goudy Old Style
by HBM Typesetting, Chorley, Lancs.
Printed and bound in Italy by Sagdos SpA

British Library Cataloguing in Publication Data

Black, Maggie
   Cheesecakes—(Ward Lock cookery course)
   1. Cheesecake (Cookery)
   I. Title
   641.6'73   TX773

ISBN 0-7063-6308-6

CONTENTS

Acknowledgements

The publisher and author would like to thank the following for their co-operation and assistance in the production of this book.

For recipes:

Cadbury-Typhoo Limited Food Advisory Service
English Country Cheese Council
Farmhouse English Cheese Information Office
Judy Ridgway
Kellogg Company of Great Britain Limited
Longley Farm, Holmfirth, Yorkshire
Swiss Cheese Union
Unigate Foods (St. Ivel) Limited

For test materials:

Billingtons Natural Brown Sugars
Longley Farm (for all cottage cheese used)

Cover photograph by Edmund Goldspink
Inside photography by Edmund Goldspink and Louis Jordaan

Photographs on pages 41, 53, 57, 61 supplied courtesy of Edward Billington (Sugar) Limited, Cadbury-Typhoo Limited Food Advisory Service, Kellogg Company of Great Britain Limited **and** The Summer Orange Office respectively.

Notes

It is important to follow *either* the metric *or* the imperial measures when using these recipes.

All spoon measures are level.

Flour is plain and sugar is granulated unless otherwise specified.

INTRODUCTION

Cheesecakes are not a modern invention. They may well have been the first desserts ever made. The ancient Egyptians and Sumerians ate them. So did biblical, migrant tribes, following their flocks. In ancient Greece, wedding cakes were cheesecakes.

Those early cheesecakes were created and eaten in warm climates where fresh milk and cream soured quickly, but where grass, and therefore milk-giving animals, were common. All round the Mediterranean, from the steppe lands of south Russia and the Balkans to the Middle East, desserts made with soft cheeses are still one of the most practical ways to use the food value of whole milk; certainly for the peasant farmers, who still make their own curd cheeses as a matter of habit. A goatskin bag of soft cheese hangs outside every second cottage in any small Greek or Israeli village, and every household tent of a pastoral Arab tribe.

The cheesecakes these people make, now traditional favourite foods all over eastern Europe, are often rich, solid mixtures, made with full-fat soft cheese and cultured or soured cream; they often contain dried fruit, and are given a baked-on soured cream topping. They are usually only 5–8cm (2–3 inches) deep, and are baked in a pastry or crumb shell, so they often look more like tarts or flans. Being convenient to transport, they became characteristically Jewish foods many centuries ago, and are now familiar, well-loved desserts wherever Jewish communities have found a home.

In western Europe, especially England, a different tradition developed. In medieval days, in the dairy of any wealthy man's castle or manor, the rich milk from cows on lush pasture was often allowed to stand until the cream could be skimmed off to use for butter-making. The best of the slightly soured milk was then set as soft cheese for the lord of the manor and his lady to eat as 'white meats', especially on the many fast days imposed by the early Church. These wealthy aristocrats loved sweet foods, so cheesecakes were among the most popular 'white meats' they enjoyed. Their cheesecakes were often set with plenty of well-whisked eggs, making up for the forbidden meat.

The mixture of traditions led, in time, to the development of a new style all-American cheesecake. This is the type we generally picture when we think of a cheesecake. It is usually set on a pastry or crumb base instead of in a shell, and is up to 10cm (4 inches) deep. The mixture is generally based on full-fat soft cheese with cream added, and is lightened with whisked eggs. It may be baked but is quite likely to be set with gelatine instead. Toppings vary widely, but are nearly always colourful; jam glaze or sliced fruit are the most popular.

Some American party cheesecakes consist just of the set cheese mixture coated with crumbs. These tortes, as they are sometimes called, are served as a rich dessert with whipped cream. Like other American cheesecakes, they will often serve 12–16 people. Most American cheesecakes, for all their fragile fluffiness, are richer than they seem; their curd and egg-white lightness is deceptive.

Most of the recipes in this book are for traditional, rich cheesecakes, tarts and flans, and the fluffier American cheesecakes in all their variety. They range from rich, luxurious party cheesecakes to low-fat and economical ones, all of which are now among our most popular desserts.

PRINCIPAL INGREDIENTS

Cheeses and Curds

Most cheesecakes are made with soft cheese. All soft cheeses consist of partly-drained milk curds made from milk soured naturally or set with rennet or an acid. They may be made from whole full-fat milk, skimmed milk, or may have cream or butter added to make a richer cheese. They may be heat-treated, as cottage cheese is, to set the curd more firmly. Most soft cheeses are salted to preserve them for a short time and to give them a more interesting flavour.

In Britain soft cheeses are divided into six grades, depending on how much butterfat they have, and the Trade Descriptions Act has laid down what each grade of cheese must be called. The grades are:

less than 2% butterfat	skimmed milk soft cheese
2–10% butterfat	low-fat soft cheese
10–20% butterfat	medium-fat soft cheese
20–45% butterfat	full-fat soft cheese
45–65% butterfat	*cream cheese
over 65% butterfat	*double cream cheese

*Cream cheeses are seldom true cheeses; usually they are not made from curds, just drained, set cream.

The names *low-fat, medium-fat* and so on are now printed on the packets or cartons of most soft cheeses, foreign as well as British, so you can swap one brand for another of the same grade if you like its flavour or texture better. Go by the grade names (low-fat etc.) not the butterfat percentages, which are calculated in different ways in different countries.

One other point about soft cheese may be confusing; many of the richer, full-fat soft cheeses are what we used to call cream cheeses, and quite a number of retailers still sell them as such. Do not be misled. If you are offered cream cheese, say in a delicatessen, ask to see the label on the manufacturer's carton; the chances are that it will have 'Full-Fat Soft Cheese' written on it. Real cream cheese is rarely sold because it is too rich for most people's taste, it is expensive, and it goes off very quickly.

A few recipes for traditional cheesecakes call for the use of unsalted soft cheese. For these recipes you can sometimes get unsalted soft cheese in a health food store. An easier alternative may be to make your own so a recipe for home-made cheese which is firm, and therefore suitable, is given on page 9.

Whether you buy or make the soft cheese, it will not keep long, once made. Although soft cheeses were invented as a way of preserving milk, they are a very short-term preserve. Your cheese will get progressively sharper-flavoured every day, so use it quickly. Cheesecakes were first developed as one way of preserving soft cheese just a little longer, and in fact one of the great merits of many cheesecakes is that they can, and should, be kept for 1–2 days or even longer before use. Many cheesecakes also freeze perfectly which most soft cheeses do not; unless they are very rich in fat they go grainy.

Their keeping quality makes cheesecakes especially convenient as party desserts because you can make them ahead of time. Another good feature is that they are so adaptable; a modern cheesecake can be as rich or plain as you wish. It can also, provided the cheese is still fairly bland, be given almost any flavouring you like.

Making Soft Cheeses

Cheese is made by minute bacteria called STREPTOCOCCUS LACTIS or 'STREP LACTIS'. (Yogurt is made by similar bacteria.) STREP LACTIS occurs naturally in raw milk, but there are no bacteria in pasteurized milk; so they must be put back to make the milk turn sour and set instead of going putrid.

Some people wait for the milk to go sour naturally, with the help of STREP LACTIS from the air, but it may be risky. A surer way is to put a culture or starter of the right bacteria into the milk. The easiest way to do it is to add a rennet tablet or some yogurt to the milk, and make junket or yogurt cheese.

HOME-MADE MILK CURD CHEESE

Makes about 125g (4oz) cheese

600ml (1 pint) whole **or** skimmed milk
rennet essence **or** unflavoured rennet
tablet to set 600ml (1 pint) milk
$\frac{1}{4}$–$\frac{1}{2}$ teaspoon salt (optional)

Make a firm unsweetened junket with the milk and rennet as directed on the rennet bottle. Scald a thin square cloth or man's handkerchief. Lay it over a sieve balanced on a basin, with the corners hanging loose. Tip in the junket. Gather up the corners of the cloth, tie them together to form a bag, and hang it up to drain. After 6–8 hours, scrape down any curd on the sides of the cloth into the main mass, turn the curd over, and rehang the bag. Repeat this process after another 6–8 hours if the cheese is still wetter than you want it. When the cheese has the texture you want, add salt to taste for savoury use if desired; use very little salt for cheesecakes. Work the salt into the cheese, then pack the cheese in a carton, cover and refrigerate. Alternatively, form into a pat for immediate use. Use as a low-fat soft cheese.

Note Cream can be added to the cheese if a richer cheese is wanted.

YOGURT CHEESE

Makes about 125g (4oz) cheese

600–750ml (1–1$\frac{1}{4}$ pints) natural yogurt
salt (optional)

Drain the yogurt in the same way as junket (see previous recipe). When it has the texture you want, work in a little salt if desired, turn the cheese into a carton, and refrigerate for not more than 48 hours before use. Yogurt makes a firm, smooth cheese particularly suitable for cheesecakes. Use as a low-fat soft cheese.

Other Main Ingredients

Certain ingredients besides cheese feature regularly in cheesecakes old and new.

All baked cheesecakes and some others contain EGGS. Size 4 or 5 eggs have been used in making these recipes.

Many unbaked cheesecakes are set with GELATINE. Sometimes it is in the form of a flavoured jelly tablet which will set 600ml (1 pint) liquid. Usually, however, it is unflavoured granulated (powdered) gelatine which is sold in packets holding 15g ($\frac{1}{2}$ oz), which is 1 tablespoon.

CREAM is used in a lot of cheesecakes. It may be double cream containing at least 48% butterfat, whipping cream with at least 35% butterfat, which makes lighter cheesecakes, or single cream with a minimum of 18% butterfat. Quite a lot of recipes use soured cream (18% butterfat) because, originally, one function of cheesecakes was to preserve cream which had already soured and would soon go bad.

All the recipes in this book use standard quality cream, normally sold in waxed cartons holding 142ml (5 fl oz) and 284ml (10 fl oz) in Britain. U.H.T. (ultra heat treated) cream, which keeps for months on the shelf in its sealed waxed carton, is just as suitable as ordinary short-lived pasteurized cream. Whipping cream is particularly useful to keep in this form. Its 35–42% butterfat makes it a better consistency for whipping than double cream, and the heat treatment does not destroy the flavour of the fresh cream. Sterilized creams which are longer-lived have an altered flavour.

Eastern European and Balkan cheesecakes, and some modern American ones, are often made with natural (unflavoured) YOGURT instead of soured cream. Almost all the yogurt sold commercially today is low-fat yogurt made from skimmed milk, and so the recipes in this book have been adapted to use it.

A point to notice about the yogurt in all these recipes is that it is treated as a liquid; the quantity to use is given in millilitres, and in fractions of a pint or fluid ounces. Some, although not all, commercial yogurt is sold by weight, in grams or ounces. So it is always wise to measure the yogurt in a measuring jug before using it. Stir it gently to liquefy it before measuring.

Another point to watch is the sell-by date on the carton. Fresh yogurt should always be used for cheesecakes if possible. Any yogurt gets more acid day by day and may be too acid for a cheesecake by the end of its shelf life.

Most cheesecakes have at least a hint of LEMON flavouring to give them a tang. As a rule, the flavour of the cheese should dictate just how much lemon tang it needs, so most recipes simply tell you to use the juice and/or rind of $\frac{1}{2}$ or 1 lemon; the size of lemon is left to you. As a guide, however, the recipes throughout this book have used whole lemons weighing 90g (3 oz) each.

For cheesecakes which contain only lemon juice, without rind, unsweetened bottled or canned lemon juice can be used instead of fresh juice. Use 2 tablespoons of juice instead of each whole lemon. As a rule, bottled or canned juice does not need straining. Fresh juice should only be strained if you want a very smooth cheesecake filling; otherwise, the minute fragments of lemon flesh give it an interesting texture.

As for the rind, grate off just the thin yellow outer skin which contains the flavouring oil or zest. The white pith underneath is bitter.

Many traditional cheesecakes contain DRIED FRUIT as well as lemon. Raisins or sultanas, once called golden raisins, are the most usual dried fruit in these cheesecakes. Stoned and seedless raisins are both widely available in packets, ready washed and dried. Stoned raisins are larger and juicier but they may be too heavy in a light cheesecake, so they are best kept for the creamier, denser fillings. Seedless raisins, which are smaller and cheaper, do just as well if you soak them in boiling water for a short time. However, it is most important to pat them dry thoroughly before using them; wet raisins in a cheesecake are disastrous.

Modern dessert cheesecakes have many other fruit flavourings, using WHOLE FRUIT or only juice. Whole fruit may be fresh, frozen or canned. It may be used sliced under the filling mixture or placed on top; or it may be made into an almost set purée or glaze. Fresh fruit almost always has a more vital flavour, but canned fruit is more vivid and is available all year round. Make sure that all fruit is really well drained; if not it will make a soggy mess of the cheesecake filling or crust under it. Fresh fruit in cheesecakes usually has sugar added. Canned fruit may be in its own juice or in syrup, and either may be added to the cheesecake mixture for extra flavour.

Some cheesecakes are almost unsweetened; others are very sweet, especially if made with fruit syrup. Cheesecakes are normally sweetened with white SUGAR. Brown sugar makes them dingy instead of deliciously snowy-white or lemon-gold, and the flavour of the brown sugar may mask the clean, fresh taste of the cheese and lemon. However, you can use a light muscovado or similar brown sugar for any cheesecake if you wish. Honey, although deliciously flavoured, may be hazardous to use unless a recipe is designed for it; it changes the consistency of the mixture, and may give it a sticky texture if used in any quantity.

Cheesecakes may have many other ingredients to give them firmness, colour or flavour. Originally, wholemeal, rye or potato flour was used for traditional cheesecakes, but today WHITE FLOUR is almost always used for both pastry crusts and fillings, for lightness. SPICES and NUTS give flavour and texture to the older, more solid cheesecakes. The more delicate, fluffier modern ones may contain a LIQUEUR teamed with fruit to make them luxury desserts.

Bases, Coverings and Sauces

Pastry and Sponges

Many cheesecakes, especially the traditional rich ones from eastern Europe, are baked in a pastry case or shell. Any standard pastry suitable for sweet dishes may be used except flaky and choux pastry. Large or heavy cheesecakes need a solid casing which will not crack when removed from the baking tin. This is one reason why many traditional cheesecakes have a rich, shortcrust pastry shell. Rich pastry is also much less likely to toughen during the long cooking time that is required by a large cheesecake.

If the cheesecake filling has a distinct flavour besides that of the sweetened cheese, the pastry for its case is often flavoured to suit it. For instance, ground cinnamon or ginger may be added to the pastry flour if the filling is spicy or fruit-flavoured, or ground almonds may replace some of the flour for an almond-flavoured cheesecake.

Any pastry case, flavoured or not, may be filled while still uncooked and be baked with its filling, or it may be baked blind (see page 12) before being filled. It depends on the type of filling, how moist it is, and for how long and at what temperature it will be baked, if at all. A large cheesecake baked in a deep cake tin seldom has a pastry case, but when it does, the bottom of the case is usually baked blind first, and the uncooked sides are fitted into the tin and sealed to the baked pastry just before the filling mixture is put in.

Every pastry-cased cheesecake recipe in this book either includes the recipe for its own special pastry, or suggests the quantity and type of standard pastry to use. In each case, the pastry has been carefully chosen to suit the texture or flavour of the cheesecake. Moist or heavy fillings, especially fruit-filled ones, should always be baked in the recommended pastry. For lighter cheesecakes you can use your own favourite pastry, or bought frozen pastry for convenience. To make it easy, recipes using standard pastry give the quantity as ready-made dough.

Some pastry mixtures for casing cheesecakes are so rich or soft that they cannot be rolled out easily. This type of mixture is sometimes called a pressed pastry. A pressed pastry dough is, literally, pressed in an even layer on to the base and sides of a greased baking tin or flan case, like a crumb crust. This is usually done most easily with the back of a spoon, although an even richer, moister mixture may need to be spread with a knife. Some spreading mixtures which contain only a little flour are more like batter than pastry.

For a lighter foundation, a Genoese or similar sponge base is sometimes used instead of pastry. A sponge base is always baked and cooled before the cheesecake mixture is put on top. It makes a delicate yet firm base for a fluffy party cheesecake.

Rich Shortcrust or Flan Pastry

Makes about 250g (8oz) pastry

125g (4oz) flour
salt
40g (1½oz) margarine
40g (1½oz) lard
1 teaspoon castor sugar
1 egg
cold water as required

Sift the flour and a pinch of salt together. Rub in the fats with the fingertips, until the mixture resembles fine breadcrumbs. Mix in the sugar. Blend the egg with a few drops of water, and use to bind the mixture. Knead lightly until the dough is smooth and without cracks. Allow to stand for 10 minutes. Roll out, without stretching, on a lightly floured board. Use at once, or fold, wrap in clingfilm, and chill for up to 24 hours before use. Bake, as a rule, at 200°C, 400°F, Gas 6.

To Line and Bake a Pastry Case Blind

Grease the inside of a sandwich cake tin, flan case or flan ring set on a heavy baking sheet. Roll out the pastry on a lightly floured board. Lift it on the rolling pin, and lay it on the tin. Lift the edges of the pastry, and lower the centre portion on to the base of the tin. Ease the pastry into the tin to cover the whole base. Press it lightly into the angle between the base and sides, and up the sides. Cut off any excess pastry at the top edge of the tin, or make a decorative fluted edge around the top. Prick the base of the pastry lightly with a fork. Cut out a circle of greaseproof paper slightly larger than the tin, grease it lightly and fit it into the tin, greased side down. Fill it with dried beans or rice. Bake for 10–15 minutes at 190°C, 375°F, Gas 5, or at the main recipe temperature, until it is firm and just beginning to brown at the top. Remove the beans or rice and the paper, and return to the oven for 5 minutes to dry out the base of the case. Cool if necessary and use as required, or store for up to 48 hours in an airtight tin before use.

To Bake a Pastry Case in a Deep Cake Tin

You will need nearly twice as much pastry as for a flan ring of the same diameter; the exact quantity will depend on the depth of the tin.

Roll out the pastry on a lightly floured board, and cut out a round which will fit the base of the tin. Cut out separately a strip or strips which will fit the sides of the tin. Keep these strips aside. Turn the tin upside down, and grease the underside of the base lightly. Lay the pastry round on it. Put in the oven and bake at the main recipe temperature until the pastry is firm but not yet browned. Cool. Remove the pastry, and turn the tin right way up. Lightly grease the inside of the tin. Lay the baked pastry round in the base, and dampen the edges with water. Fit the uncooked pastry strips round the sides, sealing them to the baked base with light pressure. Fill with the chosen filling, and bake as the recipe requires.

Crumb Crusts and Coatings

Modern cheesecakes more often have a crumb crust than a pastry shell or base. The crust is not a top covering, but a crusty layer or shell made of ready-baked fine bread, biscuit or cake crumbs mixed with fat and with sugar (for plain crumbs). It supports the cheesecake exactly like a pastry base.

As a rule plain or sweet biscuit crumbs are used to make crumb crusts for cheesecakes. Digestive biscuit crumbs are most popular because of their semi-sweet, slightly nutty flavour, but there are many other interesting kinds as illustrated in the table opposite.

Consider the flavour and texture of your cheesecake or topping before deciding what type of crumbs to use. Sharp-flavoured fruit cheesecakes, such as redcurrant or apricot ones, usually need a smooth crust of plain biscuit crumbs made with Marie or similar biscuits. Classic lemon cheesecakes, however, welcome the contrasting texture of digestive or gingernut crumbs. A spicy cheesecake will take the more insistent flavour of crispbreads or oatcakes, while a fragile, luxurious party cheesecake is best on a smooth, sweet crust. Every crumb-based cheesecake recipe in this book suggests a type of crumb that is suitable, but you may use another type if you prefer.

Crumbs are all made in the same way. Break up biscuits, crispbreads or cookies roughly. Put the pieces between two sheets of stout paper; the top sheet is needed to prevent the crumbs scattering. Roll a heavy rolling pin or bottle over the top sheet of paper. Remove any rice paper from macaroon crumbs, and any hard or lumpy bits from other biscuits, and roll again until the crumbs are fine and even. Tip them into a jar with an airtight lid, and store on the shelf or in the refrigerator, until they are required for use.

Any crumb crust is bound with softened or melted fat. Almost always, butter, margarine or melted chocolate is used, depending on the flavour of the cheesecake and crumbs; hard margarine or soft tub margarine is equally suitable.

As a rule, unflavoured, dry and slightly sweetened crumbs have sweetening added. The commonest sweetening is sugar but you can use honey, jam, golden syrup, treacle or molasses if you wish. Take care not to make the mixture sticky or it may 'weep' later, and will stick to the tin and be messy to cut when served.

BISCUITS TO USE FOR CRUMB CRUSTS

Type of biscuit	Crumbs
water biscuits, cream crackers	smooth, unflavoured, unsweetened, dry
wheat crispbreads, rusks	slightly grainy, nutty-flavoured, unsweetened, dry
oatcakes (plain or sweetened), bran biscuits, some crispbreads	grainy, nutty-flavoured, unsweetened or semi-sweet, dry
plain biscuits such as Marie, Butter Osborne, Rich Tea and most breakfast food flakes	smooth, slightly sweetened, dry
sweet biscuits such as Lincoln, Petit Beurre	smooth, sweet, no marked flavour, dry
sweet flavoured biscuits such as gingernuts, spice biscuits	smooth, sweet, marked flavour, dry
shortbreads, digestive biscuits, chocolate biscuits, chocolate digestive biscuits (plain or milk), oatmeal parkin	smooth or slightly grainy, semi-sweet or sweet, flavoured, rich
macaroons, peanut and other nut biscuits	grainy or fibrous, full-flavoured, rich

A variety of interesting crusts may be made by adding flavouring, or ingredients which change the crust's texture. Try ground cinnamon or mace, allspice, mixed spice or grated nutmeg for a spiced crust. Add crushed wheat, grated or finely chopped nuts, desiccated or toasted coconut, sesame seeds or soaked poppy seeds for texture interest.

All crumb crusts are prepared as follows: The crumbs are mixed with any other dry ingredients, and the fat is worked in with a fork or the back of a spoon, to make a crumbly or a pasty mixture. A liquid sweetening is usually worked in with the fat. The mixture is then pressed or spread over the base, or the base and sides, of the cake tin, flan case, flan ring or pie plate in which the cheesecake is to be baked or chilled. A cake tin should have a removable base, and any container should be well greased inside, or, better still, be lined with greased paper before putting in the crumb mixture. The crust is then chilled to firm it up, or it may be baked for 8–10 minutes to crisp it. A moist cheesecake is best on a pre-baked crust to avoid any risk of it being soggy.

When you line a flan case or ring completely with a crumb crust, make the sides the same thickness all the way up; when pressing the mixture into place, one can easily make the sides too thin and fragile at the top so that they crumble. When the case is complete, slice off any bits of crust which stick up, using a sharp knife held horizontally. Then brush off any loose crumbs on the top and inside of the case.

However, if you make a base and a shallow 2.5cm (1 inch) rim to support a higher cheesecake mixture, make the top edge as thin as you can, to avoid biting into a doorstep of crust near the base of the cheesecake.

Some dessert cheesecakes, especially party ones, do not have a solid base at all. Instead, they have a thin coating of crumbs sprinkled all over the inside of a well-greased container before the filling mixture is put in. Only 30–40g (1–1½ oz) of crumbs are needed, even for a big cake tin.

Another, and decorative, way to use crumbs on a cheesecake is to press them gently with your palms on to the sides of an unbaked cheesecake after removing the container. The pressure must be gentle and the crumbs fairly fine since some of these cheesecakes are fragile. Finely chopped or ground nuts, or desiccated coconut can also be used in the same way.

Toppings and Sauces

GOLDEN OATMEAL TOPPING

Covers 2×18cm (7 inch) cheesecakes

90g (3 oz) butter
150g (5 oz) dry white breadcrumbs
30g (1 oz) coarse oatmeal
60g (2 oz) sugar
½ teaspoon ground cinnamon
¼ teaspoon grated nutmeg

Melt the butter in a large frying pan. Stir in the breadcrumbs and oatmeal, and turn them over in the butter until light gold and crisp. Stir in the sugar and spices, scrape together and turn on to a baking sheet. Spread out in an even layer, and cool. Then store in an airtight jar, refrigerated, until needed. The topping keeps for 2–3 weeks. Use instead of biscuit or cake crumbs for sprinkling on strongly lemon-flavoured, tangy or slightly spicy cheesecakes.

CHOCOLATE CURLS FOR DECORATING

Chill a solid block of chocolate until cold and hard. Shave it in long strokes with a vegetable peeler or on the broad slicing blade of a box grater. The shavings will come off as long thin curls. Handle them with care; they are fragile, and should be as long and curly as possible for their best effect.

For broader chocolate curls, or scrolls, break up the chocolate and melt it on a plate over a pan of simmering water. Leave the chocolate to cool on the plate or spread it on an oiled stone or formica slab until almost set. Scrape off broad curls with a sharp knife held almost horizontally against the chocolate. These broad curls are also called chocolate caraque.

Chill the curls, then pile them lightly on a cheesecake just before serving.

BLACKCURRANT PURÉE FOR TOPPING OR SAUCE

Serves 4–6

1×485g (1 lb 1½ oz) can **or** jar blackcurrants in syrup
2 teaspoons crème de cassis liqueur (optional)

Drain the fruit and reserve 175ml (6 fl oz) of the syrup; you will probably need all the syrup from a can or jar. Turn the fruit and syrup into a saucepan, and simmer for 4 minutes. Cool slightly, then process in an electric blender if possible, before sieving; this gives a thicker purée than if the fruit is only sieved. Stir in the liqueur if used, pour into a carton or jug, cover and chill until required. Reheat gently if desired in a heatproof jug standing in a bain-marie.

Variations

Other Soft Fruit Purées
Use other soft fruits, alone or mixed, instead of blackcurrants. Blackberries, elderberries, loganberries, raspberries, redcurrants, strawberries or plums all make good purées. Mulberries do not have enough flavour.

If using a liqueur, suit it to the flavour of the fruit. Use crème de cassis with blackberries or elderberries; framboise, kirsch or Cointreau with loganberries, raspberries, redcurrants or strawberries, and mirabelle with plums.

MELBA SAUCE

Covers 1×15cm (6 inch) cheesecake or
4 individual helpings

250g (8 oz) fresh ripe raspberries
2–4 tablespoons white wine, not too dry
3 tablespoons icing sugar or to taste

Hull and pick over the fruit and spread it on a plate. Sprinkle with 2 tablespoons of the wine and the icing sugar. Leave for 30 minutes, then sieve the fruit and any juice with it into a heatproof bowl. Taste, and add the remaining wine and more icing sugar if you wish. Balance the bowl over a pan of simmering water, and stir for 2 minutes. Cool, then chill before using.

APRICOT GLAZE

Makes about 400g (14 oz) glaze for storage

500g (1 lb) apricot jam
2 tablespoons lemon juice
2 tablespoons cold water

Warm the jam slightly, then sieve it into a clean saucepan. Add the other ingredients, and stir over gentle heat until the jam dissolves. Simmer for 4 minutes. While simmering, rinse out a heatproof jar with boiling water. Turn the glaze into the wet jar, cover with a disc of waxed paper and cool. Use a few spoonfuls when tepid and still liquid if needed at once, then cool the rest completely, and cover with an airtight lid or cover like jam. To use stored glaze, reheat by standing the container in very hot water. Cool to tepid before using.

To use, spoon or paint the glaze over the surface of a cheesecake, or over fruit arranged in a decorative pattern on the top.

Variations

Redcurrant Glaze
Use redcurrant jelly instead of apricot jam.
Somerset Glaze
Use apple or crab-apple jelly instead of apricot jam.
Scots Glaze
Use fine shred jelly marmalade (orange or lemon) and 2 teaspoons whisky instead of apricot jam.
Welsh Glaze
Use rowan jelly instead of apricot jam.

APRICOT SAUCE

Makes about 400ml (¾ pint) sauce

250g (8oz) dried apricots
cold water as required
90g (3oz) light soft brown sugar
salt
1 tablespoon orange juice
1–2 tablespoons Cointreau (optional)

Steep the apricots overnight in enough cold water to cover them by 3cm (1½ inches). Put both in a saucepan, half cover and simmer until the fruit is pulpy; add a very little more water if you need to. Sieve or blend both fruit and liquid. Put back in the saucepan, add the sugar and a pinch of salt and stir over gentle heat until the sugar melts. Cool, then add the orange juice and the liqueur if used. Measure and add water to make the sauce up to 400ml (¾ pint), or to taste. Reheat, or chill to use cold.

GINGER AND APRICOT TOPPING OR SAUCE

Makes about 300ml (½ pint) sauce
Covers 1×18cm (7 inch) cheesecake

boiling water as required
90g (3oz) dried apricots
30g (1oz) preserved stem ginger in syrup
100ml (4floz) whipping cream
2–3 drops lemon juice **or** to taste

Pour plenty of boiling water over the apricots and leave over-night. Drain them thoroughly, then sieve or blend them until smooth. Drain the ginger, reserving the syrup, and chop it very finely. Mix with the apricot purée. Whip the cream until it just holds soft peaks, gradually adding 2 tablespoons reserved syrup and 1–2 drops lemon juice. Fold the apricot and ginger mixture into the cream, taste and add extra lemon juice if you wish. Chill before using.

PINEAPPLE TOPPING

Makes about 80–100ml (3–4floz)
Covers 1×23cm (9 inch) cheesecake

125g (4oz) canned crushed pineapple
40g (1½oz) castor sugar **or** to taste
2 tablespoons cold water
1 tablespoon cornflour
½ teaspoon butter
1–2 drops yellow food colouring

Drain the fruit well and process in an electric blender until fairly smooth. Put in a saucepan with the sugar and water. Blend the cornflour to a smooth paste with a little of the mixture, then stir it into the rest of the mixture. Taste and add extra sugar if you wish. Heat very gently, stirring constantly, until the glaze boils and thickens. Stir in the butter and food colouring, and let the butter melt. Pour into a cold container. Spoon over a cheesecake when the topping is almost or quite cold.

LEMON SAUCE

Makes about 400ml (¾ pint) sauce

rind ½ lemon
300ml (½ pint) cold water
90g (3oz) castor sugar
80ml (3floz) lemon juice
2 teaspoons arrowroot
2 drops yellow food colouring
3 tablespoons medium-dry white wine
or dry sherry (optional)

Pare off the lemon rind in long strips, and steep it in the water, in a saucepan, for 20 minutes. Take it out. Add the sugar to the water, heat to the boil, and simmer, uncovered for 5 minutes. Blend 1 tablespoon of the lemon juice with the arrowroot to make a smooth cream. Remove the pan from the heat, stir in the remaining lemon juice and the food colouring, then stir in the arrowroot cream. Heat again, still stirring, until the sauce thickens and clears. Stir in the wine or sherry if used. Cool, covered, before use.

FRESH STRAWBERRY TOPPING

Makes about 300ml (½pint) sauce
Covers 2×23cm (9inch) cheesecakes

250g (8oz) fresh strawberries
125g (4oz) castor sugar
4 tablespoons cold water
salt
1½ tablespoons cornflour
1 teaspoon butter

First hull the strawberries, then slice and sieve them, or process in an electric blender. Turn into a small saucepan, and mix in the sugar, water and a few grains of salt. Blend a little of the mixture with the cornflour to make a smooth paste, then combine the paste with the rest of the mixture, taking care not to leave any lumps. Stirring continuously, bring slowly to the boil, and continue stirring until the mixture thickens. Stir in the butter. Skim, and pour into a clean container. Spoon over a cheesecake when the topping has almost completely cooled, or store it in a refrigerator or freezer.

To use from storage first bring to room temperature. Then put in a heatproof bowl over a pan of very hot water, and stir until just liquid.

TOASTED FLAKED ALMONDS

For crumb crusts, and for decorating the tops and sides of cheesecakes

1 tablespoon frying oil
125g (4oz) flaked almonds

Warm the oil in a large frying pan, tilting the pan to film the base. Tip the nuts and spread them in as thin a layer as possible. Place over very gentle heat, and turn the nuts over continuously with a metal spatula or spoon until they are golden; do not stop turning them, or they will burn almost instantly. Turn them on to absorbent kitchen paper and pat dry. Leave to cool, then store in a jar with a screwtop lid. The nuts can be crushed to crumbs for covering the sides of a cheesecake.

Hints on Baking and Chilling Cheesecakes

Baked cheesecakes often behave like soufflés. They rise dramatically while being baked, then sink ignominiously when taken out of the oven. After two or three such experiences, it is tempting to leave a cheesecake in the oven for 5–10 minutes longer than the stated time, to set it more firmly. This is usually a mistake; the cheesecake still falls, and is tough through overbaking. It is better to underbake a cheesecake slightly, i.e. to turn off the oven heat when it is only just set. Even more important, almost any cheesecake should be cooled very slowly. As a general rule, never take a cheesecake out of a hot oven into a cold draughty atmosphere, dump it on a cold surface or remove the tin and let cold air circulate round it while it is still hot. Many recipes for baked cheesecakes in this book direct you to cool the cheesecake in the turned-off oven with the door ajar. Always, in fact, do this unless some other specific direction is given. Even if the cheesecake does still sink – and most do – it will be less dense in texture and will crack less than if cooled suddenly.

Many cheesecakes crack as they cool. Do not worry about this. They may look less glamorous, but their flavour is not affected. For party use, a fruit topping or rosettes of cream will cover the cracks.

A cheesecake baked or chilled for the correct time to set it lightly may still seem wobbly or moist if the tin or mould is then removed at once. Again, one may be tempted to bake it longer or blame the recipe for not including enough gelatine. The mistake, however, is in removing the tin or mould too soon. Almost all cheesecakes firm up considerably during the 24 hours after being made, and as a general rule, all cheesecakes should be kept for 24 hours in the refrigerator or a cold larder before being served. In this book, special directions to serve at once are given for any cheesecake which should be served as soon as it is made. All other cheesecakes should be kept for several hours at least before being served. If a longer storage period is needed, the recipe says so.

Freezing Cheesecakes

Plain baked cheesecakes freeze perfectly. Gelatine-set cheesecakes can be frozen unless they contain custard or a high proportion of whole eggs or fresh fruit. If they contain any of these, they will break down when thawed. Clear jelly toppings will go cloudy in storage.

Other cheesecakes should be frozen without a topping or decorations. Most nut, crumb, jam and fruit toppings can be frozen separately. Sauces to accompany the cheesecakes can also be frozen separately. Rich double cream can be frozen, whipped or unwhipped, but whipping and single cream will go grainy in storage.

Cheesecakes should be frozen without wrappings, then wrapped for storage. They should be unwrapped before thawing to avoid any risk of damaging the soft, thawed cheesecake. Baked cheesecakes generally take 3–4 hours to thaw at room temperature, unbaked cheesecakes 2–3 hours, depending on their size and contents.

Baked
Cheesecakes

Almond Sponge Cheesecake

Serves 8–10

BASE
1 tablespoon toasted flaked almonds
(see page 17)
60g (2oz) butter **or** margarine
100g (3½oz) Marie biscuit crumbs

FILLING
3×225g (8oz) packets Philadelphia soft cheese
4 egg whites
175g (6oz) castor sugar
½ teaspoon vanilla essence
almond essence

TOPPING
250ml (8floz) soured cream
1 tablespoon castor sugar
½ teaspoon vanilla essence
2 tablespoons toasted flaked almonds
(see page 17)

Line and grease the base of a 20cm (8 inch) loose-based or springform cake tin about 7.5cm (3 inches) deep. Crush the nuts and melt the fat gently. Put 2 tablespoons of the biscuit crumbs aside, and mix the rest of the crumbs and the nuts with the melted fat until well blended. Press the mixture evenly all over the base of the cake tin. Dust the sides of the tin with the reserved crumbs. Chill while making the filling.

Bring the cheese up to room temperature and soften thoroughly by mashing it with a fork. Whisk the egg whites until stiff and glossy, gradually adding the sugar, vanilla essence and a few drops of almond essence. Combine with the cheese lightly, and turn on to the chilled base. Bake at 180°C, 350°F, Gas 4, for 25 minutes. While baking, mix together the cream, sugar and vanilla essence for the topping. Spread the sour cream mixture over the hot, baked cheesecake. Raise the oven heat to 240°C, 475°F, Gas 9, return the cheesecake to the oven and bake for 5 minutes only.

Cool the cheesecake in the tin. Sprinkle with the nuts and chill for 2 hours. Run a sharp knife round the edge of the cheesecake to loosen it. Remove from the tin and serve with Melba sauce (see page 15) if desired.

PLUM CHEESECAKE

Serves 6

BASE
30g (1oz) margarine **or** butter
140g (4½oz) digestive biscuit crumbs
250g (8oz) fresh, stewed **or** canned plums

FILLING
1×225g (8oz) packet Philadelphia soft cheese
60g (2oz) margarine
2 tablespoons clear honey
150ml (¼ pint) soured cream
2 eggs, separated
grated rind and juice 1 lemon

TOPPING
150ml (¼pint) natural yogurt
1 tablespoon clear honey
1 tablespoon lemon juice

Line the base and grease the inside of a 23cm (9 inch) loose-based cake tin. Melt the fat and work in the crumbs. Press the mixture evenly over the base of the tin. Stone the plums and place on top of the base. Chill while making the filling.

First bring the cheese up to room temperature. Cream the margarine and honey together until light and fluffy. Gradually beat in the cheese, cream, egg yolks, lemon rind and juice. Whisk the egg whites until stiff and fold into the cheese mixture. Pour on to the prepared base and bake for 1 hour at 180°C, 350°F, Gas 4, until set and turning golden-brown. Reduce the oven to 150°C, 300°F, Gas 2.

For the topping beat together the yogurt, honey and lemon juice. Pour over the top of the cheesecake and smooth with a palette knife. Bake for a further 15 minutes until set. Cool in the turned-off oven with the door ajar for 30 minutes. Remove the tin before serving.

CREAMY WALNUT CHEESECAKE

Serves 10

BASE AND TOPPING
30g (1oz) walnut pieces
200g (7oz) digestive biscuit crumbs
½ teaspoon ground cinnamon
100g (3½oz) butter **or** margarine

FILLING
2×225g (8oz) packets Philadelphia soft cheese
2 large eggs
175g (6oz) castor sugar
¼ teaspoon salt
2 teaspoons vanilla essence
¼ teaspoon almond essence
400ml (¾pint) soured cream

Line the base and grease the inside of a 20cm (8 inch) loose-based sandwich cake tin. Finely chop the nuts. Mix together the crumbs, nuts and cinnamon. Melt the fat and work the dry ingredients into it. Put 3 tablespoons of the crumb-nut mixture aside for the topping, and press the rest evenly all over the base of the tin. Chill while making the filling.

First bring the cheese up to room temperature. Beat the eggs until liquid. Gradually beat them into the cheese. Add the sugar, salt and both essences. Beat until smooth. Stir in the cream, and pour the mixture on to the chilled base. Bake at 190°C, 375°F, Gas 5, for 25–30 minutes or until just set in the centre. Cool in the turned-off oven with the door ajar for 30 minutes. Remove from the oven and finish cooling completely in the tin, then chill for 12–18 hours before use. To serve, remove from the tin and sprinkle with the reserved crumbs and nuts. This cheesecake remains soft and creamy inside.

Plum Cheesecake

CREAMY CROWD CHEESECAKE

Serves 12

BASE AND TOPPING
175g (6oz) crushed cornflake crumbs
40g (1½oz) castor sugar
90g (3oz) soft tub margarine

FILLING
3×225g (8oz) packets Philadelphia soft cheese
1×200g (7oz) can sweetened condensed milk
4 eggs, separated
300ml (½pint) soured cream
1 tablespoon castor sugar
1 teaspoon vanilla essence
1 teaspoon grated orange rind
½ teaspoon salt

Line the base and grease the inside of a 25cm (10 inch) spring-form cake tin. Mix the crumbs and sugar with the margarine to make a mixture like breadcrumbs. Put half aside. Press the rest evenly over the base of the tin.

To make the filling, first bring the cheese up to room temperature. Then, using an electric mixer if possible, beat the cheese and condensed milk together until smooth. Add the yolks one at a time, blending each in thoroughly. When completely blended, beat in the cream, sugar, vanilla essence and orange rind. Separately beat the egg whites with the salt until they hold soft peaks. Fold them into the cheese mixture. Turn gently into the cake tin and sprinkle the top with the reserved crumb mixture. Bake at 150°C, 300°F, Gas 2, for 1¾–2 hours, or until a skewer run into the centre of the cake comes out clean. Cool in the turned-off oven with the door ajar. Leave in the tin until quite cold.

Serve this golden-topped cheesecake with double the recipe quantity of apricot sauce (see page 16) in a separate jug.

SNOWY PARTY CHEESECAKE

Serves 8–10

BASE
30g (1oz) gingernut crumbs

FILLING
3×225g (8oz) packets Philadelphia soft cheese
1 teaspoon vanilla essence
4 egg whites
150g (5oz) castor sugar

TOPPING
pineapple topping (see page 16)

Generously grease the inside of a 20cm (8 inch) springform cake tin. Sprinkle the crumbs over the base and sides, pressing them on firmly. To make the filling, bring the cheese up to room temperature. Cream the cheese and vanilla essence together until soft. Separately, whisk the egg whites until foamy, then whisk in the sugar gradually, beating well after each addition. Continue whisking until the whites are stiff and glossy. Fold them into the cheese mixture. Turn gently into the cake tin. Bake at 180°C, 350°F, Gas 4, for 25 minutes. The centre will still be soft. Cool slowly, in the turned-off oven with the door ajar. Then refrigerate for at least 4 hours before removing from the tin. Top with the pineapple topping (see page 16) just before serving.

This cheesecake is very white, light and moist. Cut it with a thin, sharp paring knife.

FRIDGE-FRESH CHEESECAKE

Serves 8

BASE

15g (½oz) crushed cornflake crumbs

FILLING

4×225g (8oz) packets Philadelphia soft cheese
grated rind and juice ½ lemon
150g (5oz) castor sugar
3 eggs
1 teaspoon vanilla essence

Using butter, generously grease the inside of a 20cm (8 inch) loose-based cake tin, and coat with the crumbs. Bring the cheese up to room temperature and strain the lemon juice. Put all the filling ingredients in a large bowl and beat briskly until smooth. Turn the mixture gently into the cake tin and stand it in a baking tin containing about 1cm (½ inch) of water. Bake for 1½ hours at 170°C, 325°F, Gas 3. Cool in the turned-off oven for 30 minutes. Finish cooling in the tin, then chill until needed. The cheesecake will keep for at least 2 weeks, refrigerated. Remove from the tin and decorate as desired before serving.

SWEET BRIE CHEESECAKE

Serves 8–10

BASE

125g (4oz) butter
125g (4oz) flour
60g (2oz) castor sugar

FILLING

2×225g (8oz) packets Philadelphia soft cheese
200g (7oz) soft Brie cheese
1 tablespoon flour
90g (3oz) castor sugar
4 eggs, separated
100ml (4floz) double cream
1 teaspoon vanilla essence
¼ teaspoon salt

To make the case, separately grease the base and sides of a 23cm (9 inch) loose-based cake tin about 7.5cm (3 inches) deep. Soften the butter. Mix together the flour and sugar, and work in the butter to make a soft dough. Spread half the dough evenly over the base of the tin. Bake at 200°C, 400°F, Gas 6, for 8 minutes, until lightly browned. Cool. Fit the base and sides of the tin together. Spread the remaining dough over 5cm (2 inches) of the sides of the tin, to form a shell. Chill while making the filling.

Bring the cheeses up to room temperature and remove the rind from the Brie. Beat together until very smooth and creamy. Beat in the flour and sugar. Beat in the egg yolks, one at a time, followed by the cream and vanilla essence. Separately, beat the egg whites and salt until fairly stiff. Fold into the creamy cheese mixture. Pour into the chilled case and bake at 180°C, 350°F, Gas 4, for 45 minutes. Turn off the oven and leave the cheesecake for 45 minutes longer. Then remove from the oven and cool in the tin. Remove the tin, and chill for at least 2 hours before serving.

Two-Way Cheesecake

Serves 6–8

BASE
60g (2oz) butter
250g (8oz) digestive biscuit crumbs
30g (1oz) castor sugar
1½ teaspoons ground cinnamon

FILLING
2 tablespoons cold water
1 packet (15g/½oz) gelatine } for an unbaked cheesecake

3 eggs, separated
125g (4oz) castor sugar
350g (12oz) full-fat soft cheese
(for a rich cake), **or** cottage cheese
(for a light cake)
grated rind and juice 1 lemon
150ml (¼pint) double cream (for a rich cake),
or single cream (for a light cake)
30g (1oz) chopped mixed nuts (for a
baked cheesecake)
walnut halves, glacé cherries, angelica leaves
and whipped cream for decorating an
unbaked cheesecake (optional)

Line the base and generously grease the inside of an 18cm (7 inch) loose-based cake tin. Melt the butter and work in 175g (6oz) of the crumbs, with the sugar and cinnamon. Press evenly all over the base of the tin. Coat the sides of the tin with the remaining dry crumbs. Chill while making the filling.

For an unbaked cheesecake, put the water in a small heat-proof bowl, sprinkle on the gelatine and allow to soften. Stand the bowl in a pan of very hot water, and stir until the gelatine dissolves. Leave to cool to tepid. Meanwhile beat the egg yolks and sugar together in a second heatproof bowl until well blended. Place the bowl over a pan of simmering water, and whisk until the mixture is light and creamy. Remove from the heat and continue whisking until the mixture has cooled to tepid. Sieve the cheese and stir it in with the lemon rind and juice. Whip the cream until it just holds soft peaks, and stir it lightly into the cheese mixture. Whisk the egg whites to a soft foam. Stir the cooled gelatine into the cheese mixture slowly, taking care that no lumps form, then fold in the egg whites. Turn the mixture gently on to the crumb base, and chill until set. Remove from the tin, and decorate as you wish just before serving.

For a baked cheesecake, beat the egg yolks and sugar together until thick and creamy. Sieve the cheese and beat it in with the lemon rind and juice, and the cream. Whisk the egg whites to a soft foam. Fold them into the mixture. Bake at 170°C, 325°F, Gas 3, for 45 minutes. Sprinkle the nuts on top, and bake for another 15–20 minutes. Cool in the turned-off oven with the door ajar. When cold, remove from the tin and leave in a cool place for 2 hours to firm up before serving.

Two-way Cheesecake (baked)

LIGHT CREAM CHEESECAKE

Serves 8–10

BASE AND TOPPING
175g (6oz) water biscuit crumbs
30g (1oz) castor sugar
½ teaspoon ground cinnamon
1 tablespoon butter **or** margarine

FILLING
500g (1lb) full-fat soft cheese
2 tablespoons flour
90g (3oz) castor sugar
salt
¼ teaspoon vanilla essence
4 eggs, separated
250ml (8fl oz) single cream
grated rind 1 lemon

Line the base and grease the inside of a 23cm (9 inch) loose-based cake tin. Make sure the crumbs are crushed finely and evenly, and mix them with the sugar and cinnamon. Soften the fat and gradually work it into the dry ingredients. Put aside a quarter of the crumb mixture and press the rest, in a thin even layer, over the base of the tin. Chill while making the filling.

Using an electric mixer if possible, blend the cheese, flour, sugar, a pinch of salt and the vanilla essence. Add the egg yolks one at a time, blending well each time. Then beat in the cream and lemon rind. Separately, whisk the egg whites until stiff, then fold them into the cheese mixture. Turn the mixture into the cake tin, and sprinkle with the reserved crumb mixture. Bake at 170°C, 325°F, Gas 3, for 1 hour, or until a skewer run into the centre of the cake comes out clean. Cool in the tin. Run a sharp knife round the inside of the tin to loosen the cheesecake, then remove the sides of the tin. Since this cheesecake is fragile serve it from the base of the cake tin.

CANDLELIGHT CHEESECAKE

Serves 8

BASE
60g (2oz) butter
175g (6oz) plain biscuit **or** wheat
crispbread crumbs
30g (1oz) castor sugar

FILLING AND TOPPING
200g (7oz) dried apricots
300ml (½pint) water
60g (2oz) walnut pieces
600g (1¼lb) full-fat soft cheese
200g (7oz) castor sugar
grated rind and juice 1 lemon
2 large eggs
4 tablespoons soured cream
1½ tablespoons flour
30g (1oz) sugar

Soak the apricots for the filling in the water overnight.

Line the base and grease the inside of a 20cm (8 inch) loose-based cake tin. Melt the butter for the base without letting it get hot. Work in the crumbs and sugar. Press evenly all over the base of the tin. Chill while making the filling.

Drain the apricots and reserve any remaining soaking water. Put aside 90g (3 oz) of the soaked apricots and chop the rest finely. Grind the walnut pieces coarsely. Mash the cheese until soft and then beat with the castor sugar, lemon rind and juice, eggs and cream until very smooth and creamy. Stir in the flour, chopped apricots and nuts, mixing them in evenly throughout the mixture. Turn the mixture on to the chilled base. Bake at 220°C, 425°F, Gas 7, for 15 minutes. Lower the heat to 180°C, 350°F, Gas 4, and bake for another 45 minutes or until lightly set and slightly browned. Cool in the turned-off oven with the door ajar for 30 minutes. Then remove from the oven and finish cooling in the tin.

While cooling put the reserved 90g (3 oz) of apricots in a small saucepan with the 30g (1 oz) of sugar. Measure the soaking liquid and make up to 80ml (3 fl oz) with water if necessary. Add to the pan and poach the apricots for 10 minutes, or until very soft and syrupy. Cool. Just before serving, pour the apricots and syrup over the centre top of the cheesecake.

ADAPTABLE CHEESECAKE

Serves 8

BASE AND TOPPING
100g (3½oz) butter **or** margarine
250g (8oz) digestive biscuit **or**
sweet oatcake crumbs
60g (2oz) castor sugar
1½ teaspoons ground cinnamon

FILLING
3 eggs, separated
125g (4oz) castor sugar
350g (12oz) full-fat and low-fat
soft cheeses, mixed (see **Note** below)
grated rind and juice 1 lemon
150ml (¼pint) single, double **or** soured
cream, **or** a mixture

Line the base and grease the inside of a 20cm (8inch) loose-based cake tin. Melt the fat without letting it get too hot. Put the crumbs in a bowl. Add the fat and mix until the crumbs will stick together when pressed. Separately, mix together the sugar and cinnamon. Put 2 tablespoons aside, and combine the rest with the fat-covered crumbs. Press the crumb mixture evenly over the base and sides of the tin. Chill while making the filling.

Mix the egg yolks and sugar, and beat until thick and creamy. Sieve the cheeses together, using the proportions you prefer or find convenient. Mix the sieved cheeses lightly into the egg-sugar mixture. Then lightly mix in the lemon rind and juice, and the cream. Whisk the egg whites to the same consistency as the cheese mixture. Stir in 2 tablespoons, then fold in the rest. Turn the mixture gently into the chilled shell. Bake at 170°C, 325°F, Gas 3, for 45–50 minutes. Sprinkle with the reserved sugar and cinnamon, and bake 15 minutes longer. Cool in the tin. Run a sharp knife round the inside of the tin to loosen the cheesecake, and turn out for serving.

Note The higher the proportion of full-fat cheese, the richer the cheesecake will be. 125g (4oz) full-fat cheese with 250g (8oz) low-fat cheese will give a cheesecake of average richness if you use double cream. Single cream will give you a lighter cheesecake; soured cream a tangier one.

STRAWBERRY-TOPPED CHEESECAKE

Serves 8–10

BASE
125g (4oz) butter
125g (4oz) flour
40g (1½oz) castor sugar
1 teaspoon grated lemon rind
1 egg yolk

FILLING
350g (12oz) full-fat soft cheese
250g (8oz) low-fat soft cheese
125g (4oz) castor sugar
1½ tablespoons flour
1 teaspoon grated lemon rind
¼ teaspoon vanilla essence
3 eggs
1 egg yolk
2 tablespoons double cream

TOPPING
fresh strawberry topping (see page 17)
8 fresh strawberries

Line the base and grease the inside of a 23cm (9 inch) loose-based cake tin. Soften the butter. Mix together the flour, sugar and lemon rind, and work in the butter and egg yolk to make a smooth, soft, pasty dough. With the back of a spoon, pat or spread the dough over the base and about 5cm (2 inches) of the sides of the tin. Bake at 200°C, 400°F, Gas 6, for 7–8 minutes. Cool whilst making the filling.

Using an electric mixer if possible, beat both cheeses together until creamy. Beat in the sugar, flour, lemon rind, vanilla essence and eggs. Separately, blend the extra egg yolk into the cream, then beat into the cheese mixture. Pour into the cooled shell. Bake at 140°C, 275°F, Gas 1, for 1½–2 hours or until just set. Cool in the turned-off oven for 1 hour, then remove from the oven and allow to cool completely. While cooling make up half the recipe quantity of fresh strawberry topping (see page 17) and allow to cool. When the cheesecake is completely cold, halve the strawberries and arrange on top. Spoon the cold topping over the strawberries, covering the cheesecake. Chill for at least 1 hour before serving.

MERINGUE-TOPPED CHEESECAKE

Serves 6–8

BASE
1 egg
30g (1 oz) castor sugar
30g (1 oz) flour

FILLING
250g (8 oz) full-fat soft cheese
75g (2½ oz) castor sugar
salt
1 tablespoon flour
½ teaspoon vanilla essence
grated rind ½ lemon
2 egg yolks
5 tablespoons double cream
1 teaspoon milk

TOPPING
2 egg whites
¼ teaspoon cream of tartar
60g (2 oz) castor sugar

Thoroughly grease the base of a 23cm (9 inch) flan case or ring on a baking sheet. Beat together the egg and sugar until thick and pale. Fold in the flour and spread the mixture evenly over the base. Bake at 200°C, 400°F, Gas 6, for 10–12 minutes, until cooked through and slightly shrunk from the sides of the case or ring. Cool.

For the filling, mash the cheese with a fork until soft. Beat in the sugar, a pinch of salt, the flour, vanilla essence and lemon rind. Separately, beat together the egg yolks, cream and milk until the egg yolks are liquid and blended in. Then stir into the cheese mixture and beat until smooth. Turn the mixture on to the cooled sponge base in the case or ring.

For the topping, beat the egg whites and cream of tartar until stiff, adding the sugar gradually while beating. Pile the meringue all over the cheese mixture. Bake at 180°C, 350°F, Gas 4, for 25–30 minutes or until the meringue is lightly browned. Cool completely in the turned-off oven. Serve with whipped, sweetened double cream.

MARYLAND PARTY CHEESECAKE

Serves 10–12

BASE
100g (3½ oz) butter
60g (2 oz) light soft brown sugar
250g (8 oz) Rich Tea biscuit crumbs
¼ teaspoon ground cinnamon
¼ teaspoon grated nutmeg

FILLING
4 eggs, separated
250ml (8 fl oz) soured cream
1 teaspoon vanilla essence
250g (8 oz) castor sugar
60g (2 oz) flour
¼ teaspoon salt
500g (1 lb) full-fat soft cheese

Line the base and grease the inside of a 23cm (9 inch) loose-based cake tin. Melt the butter without letting it get hot. Sieve the sugar into a bowl, add the crumbs, cinnamon and nutmeg, mix, and then work into the butter. Press the crumb mixture evenly all over the base and 2.5cm (1 inch) of the sides of the cake tin. Chill while making the filling.

Beat the egg yolks until thick, and beat in the cream and vanilla essence. Mix 175g (6 oz) of the sugar with the flour and salt, and beat into the egg-cream mixture little by little. Beat in the cheese a little at a time. Whisk the egg whites until fairly stiff, adding the remaining sugar while doing so. Fold into the cheese mixture. Turn gently into the chilled case and bake at 170°C, 325°F, Gas 3, for 1 hour. Cool in the turned-off oven with the door ajar. Remove from the tin, and chill for at least 1 hour before serving. Serve with a sweet fruit sauce (see pages 15–17).

Maryland Party Cheesecake (with Blackcurrant Purée)

BRANDIED APRICOT CHEESECAKE

Serves 8

BASE
90g (3oz) flour
90g (3oz) self-raising flour
1 teaspoon ground cinnamon
90g (3oz) butter
1 tablespoon castor sugar
1 egg yolk
2 tablespoons cold water

FILLING
500g (1lb) full-fat soft cheese
4 eggs
150g (5oz) castor sugar
1 teaspoon vanilla essence
100ml (4floz) soured cream
2 tablespoons self-raising flour

TOPPING
60g (2oz) dried apricots
1 tablespoon castor sugar
brandy to cover
whipped cream to decorate

Line the base and grease the inside of a 20cm (8 inch) loose-based sandwich cake tin. Sift both quantities of flour and the cinnamon into a mixing bowl. Rub in the butter until the mixture is like fine breadcrumbs. Stir in the sugar. Separately, beat the egg yolk with the water, and mix into the dry ingredients to make a smooth dough. Add a very little extra water if needed. Roll out on a lightly floured board and use to line the cake tin. Chill while making the filling.

Beat the cheese until very soft and smooth. Separately, beat the eggs until frothy, then beat in the sugar little by little, blending completely. Beat in the vanilla essence and cream. Gradually beat the cheese into the egg mixture, blending each addition in smoothly without leaving lumps. Sprinkle with the flour and incorporate it with one last quick beating. Turn the mixture into the chilled pastry case. Bake at 180°C, 350°F, Gas 4, for 30 minutes. Lower the heat to 150°C, 300°F, Gas 2, and bake for another 15 minutes or until the filling is lightly set. Cool for 20 minutes in the turned-off oven with the door ajar. Then remove from the oven and finish cooling at room temperature. When cool remove from the tin and then refrigerate for 24 hours before topping and serving.

Make the topping while refrigerating the cheesecake. Put the apricots and sugar in a bowl, mix well and cover with brandy. Leave overnight. Then sieve all three ingredients, or process briefly in an electric blender, to obtain a smooth purée. Spread lightly on the cheesecake just before serving and top with rosettes of whipped cream.

COFFEE AND RUM CHEESECAKE

Serves 8

BASE
60g (2oz) margarine
60g (2oz) castor sugar
1 egg
60g (2oz) self-raising flour
½ teaspoon baking powder
½ teaspoon grated orange rind

FILLING
90g (3oz) butter
125g (4oz) castor sugar
2 tablespoons instant coffee powder
1 tablespoon boiling water
1 tablespoon orange juice
2 tablespoons dark rum
1 egg
60g (2oz) flour
500g (1lb) full-fat soft cheese
300ml (½pint) whipping cream

TOPPING
rum-flavoured, sweetened whipped
cream to decorate

Line the base and grease the inside of a deep 20cm (8 inch) loose-based cake tin. Soften the margarine. Beat together all the base ingredients until smooth. Spread the mixture evenly all over the base of the tin.

Cream together the butter and sugar for the filling until light and fluffy. Dissolve the coffee powder in the water and orange juice, and add the rum. Cool to tepid, then beat into the butter-sugar mixture with the egg. Beat in the flour, a little at a time to avoid making lumps.

Separately, beat the cheese until smooth and creamy. Beat in the cream, a little at a time. Stir (do not beat) about a quarter of the cheese mixture into the coffee mixture, then stir in the rest in 2 or 3 parts. Stir well until quite smooth. Turn on to the batter base. Bake at 170°C, 325°F, Gas 3, for 1–1¼ hours, or until the cheesecake is just firm in the middle. Cool in the turned-off oven. When quite cold, decorate the centre of the cheesecake with rosettes of rum-flavoured, sweetened whipped cream, and serve.

RICH BELGIAN CHEESE FLAN

Serves 4–6

BASE
1×20cm (8 inch) puff pastry flan case,
baked blind (see page 12)

FILLING
250g (8oz) full-fat soft cheese
2 eggs
grated rind and juice ½ lemon
150ml (¼ pint) double cream
40g (1½oz) castor sugar

Soften the cheese by working with the back of a spoon. Beat in the eggs, one at a time, until smoothly blended in. Strain the lemon juice and stir it in with the lemon rind, cream and sugar; do not beat in. Turn the mixture into the pastry case, and bake at 180°C, 350°F, Gas 4, for 25 minutes or until the filling is set. Leave to cool completely before serving.

DUTCH BROWN PIE

Serves 6

BASE
175g (6oz) flour
salt
90g (3oz) butter
1–2 tablespoons cold water

FILLING
500g (1lb) full-fat soft cheese
2 tablespoons icing sugar **or** to taste
ground spices to taste:
ground cardomum, ground ginger,
grated nutmeg, ground mace
and ground cloves

Buy or prepare freshly-ground spices for this old sixteenth-century Dutch cheesecake, invented at the time when the Dutch were masters of Europe's spice trade. Use them as the recipe directs.

Line the base and grease the inside of a 20cm (8 inch) loose-based sandwich layer cake tin. Sieve the flour and a pinch or salt into a bowl. Rub in the butter and mix to a firm dough with the water. Chill. Roll out on a lightly floured board and use to line the tin.

To make the filling, beat the cheese and 2 tablespoons icing sugar together until smooth. Add a good pinch each of all the spices except the cloves; use only a tiny pinch of cloves. Mix in, and taste. Then adjust the sweetness and flavourings to suit your own taste, adding enough spice to make the cheese a warm, golden-brown colour. Spoon the mixture into the pastry case, and bake at 180°C, 350°F, Gas 4, for 45 minutes. Cool in the tin. When cold, remove from the tin and serve as a spice cake, or with cream as a dessert.

SOURED CREAM CHEESECAKE

Serves 10–12

BASE
100g (3½oz) self-raising flour
125g (4oz) butter
125g (4oz) castor sugar
2 eggs
1 tablespoon milk
1 teaspoon vanilla essence

FILLING
250g (8oz) low-fat soft cheese, **or**
use half low-fat and half full-fat soft cheese
125g (4oz) castor sugar
100ml (4floz) soured cream
1 teaspoon vanilla essence
2 eggs

TOPPING
250ml (8floz) soured cream
30g (1oz) castor sugar
1 teaspoon vanilla essence

Make the filling before the base, as follows. Beat the cheese until soft and smooth, adding the sugar. Beat in the cream and vanilla essence, then the eggs, one at a time. Beat until well blended, then put aside and make the base.

Line the base and grease the inside of a 25cm (10 inch) loose-based sandwich cake tin or flan case at least 5cm (2 inches) deep. Sprinkle a little of the flour on the bottom. Cream together the butter and sugar until light and fluffy. Beat in the eggs, one at a time, then stir in the milk and vanilla essence. Beat or stir in the remaining flour, and blend thoroughly. Spread the batter over the base and sides of the tin or case, more thickly on the base. Spoon in the filling mixture. Bake at 170°C, 325°F, Gas 3, for 1 hour.

While baking, stir together the ingredients for the topping. When the cheesecake is cooked, spoon the topping over the filling and return to the oven for 5 minutes. Cool in the turned-off oven with the door ajar for 10 minutes only, then finish cooling at room temperature. Refrigerate for at least 4 hours before serving.

MAKE-AHEAD CHEESECAKE

Serves 4–6

BASE
6 trifle sponges

FILLING
500g (1lb) low-fat soft cheese
60g (2oz) butter
½ teaspoon vanilla essence
1 tablespoon cornflour
2 tablespoons top of the milk
2 eggs, separated
60g (2oz) castor sugar

Line the base and grease the inside of an 18cm (7 inch) loose-based square cake tin. Cut the trifle sponges in horizontal slices thin enough to cover the base of the tin. Lay them in the tin.

Mash the cheese with a fork to soften it. Melt the butter without letting it get hot, and mix it into the cheese smoothly with the vanilla essence. Blend the cornflour with the milk until smooth, and stir into the cheese mixture. Mix in the egg yolks and beat well until the mixture is light. Whisk the egg whites until fairly stiff and glossy, gradually whisking in the sugar. Fold the egg whites into the cheese mixture. Turn the mixture gently into the tin, and level the surface with a palette knife. Heat the oven to 230°C, 450°F, Gas 8, and put the tin in the very hot oven. Reduce the heat at once to 180°C, 350°F, Gas 4, and bake for 25–35 minutes or until the cheesecake is just firm in the centre. Cool in the turned-off oven for 10 minutes. Remove from the oven and finish cooling in the tin. Then cover loosely with foil and refrigerate for 12–18 hours until wanted for use.

ALMOND AND CINNAMON CHEESECAKE

Serves 6–8

BASE
90g (3oz) margarine
150g (5oz) fine dry wholemeal breadcrumbs
30g (1oz) ground almonds
60g (2oz) light soft brown sugar
1½ teaspoons ground cinnamon

FILLING
3 eggs, separated
125g (4oz) castor sugar
250g (8oz) full-fat soft cheese
125g (4oz) low-fat soft cheese
grated rind and juice 1 large lemon
80ml (3floz) double cream
4 tablespoons natural yogurt

TOPPING
1 teaspoon castor sugar
½ teaspoon ground cinnamon
30g (1oz) margarine
2 tablespoons chopped almonds

Melt the margarine in a large frying pan, add the breadcrumbs and stir over gentle heat until they are slightly crisp. Stir in the almonds, sugar and cinnamon. Take off the heat and leave to cool while you line and grease the base of a 20cm (8 inch) loose-based cake tin. Press the crumb mixture evenly all over the base of the tin.

To make the filling, beat the egg yolks and sugar until thick and pale. Sieve and beat in both cheeses, with the lemon rind and juice. Fold in the cream and yogurt. Whisk the egg whites until they hold soft peaks. Stir 2 tablespoons into the cheese mixture, then fold in the rest. Turn the mixture gently on to the crumb base. Bake at 180°C, 350°F, Gas 4, for 45–50 minutes, or until the cheesecake is just firm in the centre. Cover it loosely with greaseproof paper if it begins to over-brown during cooking.

While baking, make the topping. Mix the sugar and cinnamon, and flake the margarine. When the cheesecake is ready, sprinkle it with the nuts, sugar mixture and flaked margarine. Raise the oven heat to 220°C, 425°F, Gas 7, and return the cheesecake to the oven for a few moments to colour the nuts lightly. Cool in the turned-off oven with the door ajar. Remove from the tin. Leave to firm up for 2–4 hours or longer before serving.

CRUMB-NUT CHEESECAKE

Serves 6–8

BASE
90g (3oz) butter
175g (6oz) dry white breadcrumbs
60g (2oz) castor sugar
1½ teaspoons ground cinnamon

FILLING
3 eggs, separated
125g (4oz) castor sugar
500g (1lb) full-fat soft cheese
grated rind and juice 1 lemon
150ml (¼pint) soured cream

TOPPING
1 teaspoon castor sugar
½ teaspoon ground cinnamon
30g (1oz) butter
30g (1oz) chopped mixed nuts

Melt the butter for the base in a large frying pan, add the breadcrumbs, and stir over gentle heat until golden. Remove from the heat, stir in the sugar and cinnamon, and cool. Meanwhile, line the base and grease the inside of a 20cm (8 inch) loose-based cake tin. Press about two-thirds of the crumbs evenly all over the base of the tin. Put the remaining crumbs aside.

To make the filling, beat the egg yolks until liquid, add the sugar little by little, beating until creamy. Sieve the cheese and work it in lightly. Mix in the lemon rind and juice, and the cream. Whisk the egg whites until they just hold soft peaks. Stir 2 tablespoons into the cheese mixture, then fold in the rest. Turn the mixture gently on to the crumb base. Bake at 180°C, 350°F, Gas 4, for 45 minutes.

While baking, mix the sugar and cinnamon for the topping, and stir in the reserved crumbs. When the cheesecake is ready, melt the butter for the topping. Sprinkle the crumb mixture, nuts and melted butter over the top of the cheesecake. Return to the oven and bake for another 15 minutes. Cool completely in the turned-off oven with the door ajar, then refrigerate for at least 12 hours. Remove the tin before serving.

CINNAMON CRUMB CHEESECAKE

Serves 8–10

BASE AND TOPPING
175g (6oz) dry white breadcrumbs
90g (3oz) butter
60g (2oz) castor sugar
1½ teaspoons ground cinnamon
30g (1oz) chopped mixed nuts

FILLING
3 eggs, separated
125g (4oz) castor sugar
400g (14oz) full-fat soft cheese
grated rind and juice 1 lemon
150ml (¼pint) single cream

See that the breadcrumbs are loose, fine and even. Melt the butter in a frying pan, add the breadcrumbs and turn them over with a spatula until golden. Take off the heat and stir in the sugar and cinnamon. Keep aside while you grease the sides but not the base of a 20cm (8 inch) loose-based cake tin. Line the base with a circle of bakewell paper and press about two-thirds of the crumb mixture evenly all over it. Chill. Keep the remaining crumbs aside.

To make the filling, beat the egg yolks until liquid, adding the sugar slowly, and beating until thick and creamy. Sieve in the cheese, and work it in with a fork, blending thoroughly. Add the lemon rind, then strain and add the lemon juice, mixing thoroughly. Mix in the cream. Whisk the egg whites until they just hold soft peaks. Stir 2 tablespoons into the cheesecake mixture, then fold in the rest. Turn the mixture gently on to the chilled base. Bake at 180°C, 350°F, Gas 4, for 40 minutes or until just firm. Sprinkle the remaining crumbs and the nuts on top, and bake for a further 15 minutes. Cool in the tin. Run a sharp pointed knife round the inside of the tin to loosen the cheesecake from the sides. Remove the sides of the tin, leaving the cheesecake still on the base. Loosen the base from the tin carefully with the knife, and slide the cheesecake on to a serving plate.

TEN MINUTE FRENCH CHEESECAKE

Serves 4

BASE
125g (4oz) puff pastry

FILLING
125g (4oz) full-fat soft cheese
1 tablespoon clear honey
$\frac{1}{2}$ teaspoon vanilla essence

TOPPING
icing sugar

Grease a flat baking sheet, or cover with bakewell paper. Roll out the pastry on a lightly floured board into a 20 cm (8 inch) circle. Place it on the baking sheet. Bake at 220°C, 425°F, Gas 7, for 10–12 minutes. The pastry circle should have risen high, be lightly browned, and have shrunk to about 18 cm (7 inches) in diameter. Cool it on a wire rack.

While cooling, make the filling as follows. Beat the cheese until very soft, add the honey and vanilla essence, and beat until smoothly blended. Split the cooled pastry circle horizontally. Spread the filling evenly all over the bottom half. Lay the top half beside it, cut side up. Return to the oven and bake at the temperature above for 5–6 minutes, until the filling is very lightly set and the cut surface of the top half is crisp. Cool on the baking sheet; the filling will firm up as it cools. When cooled, sandwich the two halves together lightly and sprinkle the top with icing sugar. Serve with lightly whipped cream.

HONEY CHEESECAKE

Serves 6

BASE
175g (6oz) flour
salt
125g (4oz) butter
60g (2oz) icing sugar
1 egg yolk
1 tablespoon cold water

FILLING
175g (6oz) full-fat soft cheese
4 tablespoons stiff honey
2 eggs
150ml ($\frac{1}{4}$ pint) double **or** whipping cream
$\frac{1}{4}$ teaspoon grated nutmeg

TOPPING
15g ($\frac{1}{2}$oz) chopped walnuts
whipped cream to decorate

Sift the flour and a pinch of salt into a bowl. Rub in the butter with the fingertips until the mixture resembles breadcrumbs. Sift in the icing sugar, and stir. Beat the egg yolk with the water, add to the dry ingredients, and mix. Knead well to form a smooth dough and chill for 30 minutes. While chilling, grease a 20cm (8 inch) flan ring on a baking sheet, and the baking sheet under it. Roll out the pastry on a lightly floured board and use to line the flan ring. Bake blind (see page 12) at 200°C, 400°F, Gas 6.

While cooling, make the filling. Mash the cheese until soft, and beat in the honey until smooth. Separately, beat the eggs, then beat them into the cheese mixture. Stir in the cream and nutmeg. Pour the mixture into the cooked case and bake at 180°C, 350°F, Gas 4, for 20 minutes until firm. Sprinkle with the nuts and bake for another 10 minutes. Cool in the flan ring and remove it when cold. Decorate with rosettes of whipped cream before serving.

BUDGET CHEESE PIE

Serves 4

BASE
125g (4oz) water biscuit crumbs
40g (1½oz) soft tub margarine

FILLING
250g (8oz) low-fat soft cheese
1 egg, separated
4 tablespoons double cream
grated rind ½ orange **or** lemon
30g (1oz) castor sugar
15g (½oz) sultanas (optional)

TOPPING
1 thin slice fresh orange **or** lemon without rind

Line the base and grease the inside of a 15cm (6inch) pie plate. Work the crumbs into the margarine. Press the mixture evenly all over the base of the plate. Chill while making the filling.

Mix together all the filling ingredients except the egg white. When smoothly blended, whisk the egg white until stiff, and fold it in. Turn on to the chilled base and bake at 190°C, 375°F, Gas 5, for 30–35 minutes or until the filling is set. Cool in the turned-off oven with the door ajar.

To decorate, cut the fresh fruit slice from the centre to the edge, and twist it into a curled shape. Lay it in the centre of the cheesecake and serve from the plate.

SALZBURG CURD CAKE

Makes 12 cheesecake fingers

BASE
2 tablespoons Marie biscuit crumbs

FILLING
60g (2oz) butter
90g (3oz) castor sugar
2 eggs
½ teaspoon vanilla essence
250g (8oz) low-fat soft cheese
60g (2oz) self-raising flour
1 tablespoon milk
30g (1oz) sultanas

TOPPING
icing sugar

Line the base and grease the inside of a shallow baking tin about 25×15cm (10×6inches) in size. Dust the inside well with crumbs. Cream together the butter and sugar until soft and light. Beat in the eggs, one at a time, then the vanilla essence. Sieve and beat in the cheese with the flour and milk. Stir in the sultanas. Turn the mixture into the tin in an even layer, and bake at 190°C, 375°F, Gas 5, for 45 minutes or until firm and lightly browned. Leave at room temperature for 30 minutes until the cheesecake has shrunk slightly from the sides of the tin. When completely cold, dust the top of the cheesecake with icing sugar and cut into fingers for serving.

LATTICE PEEL CHEESECAKE

Serves 4–6

BASE
125g (4oz) flour
grated rind ½ lemon
2 teaspoons icing sugar
salt
90g (3oz) margarine
1 egg, separated
1 teaspoon lemon juice

FILLING
30g (1oz) chopped mixed peel
375g (13oz) low-fat soft cheese
grated rind and juice ½ lemon
60g (2oz) castor sugar
4 tablespoons soured cream
2 eggs

Grease an 18cm (7 inch) sandwich layer tin or pie plate. Make a rich pastry with the base ingredients as follows: mix the flour, lemon rind, icing sugar and a small pinch of salt in a bowl. Rub in the margarine as finely as possible. Mix together the egg yolk and lemon juice, and add to the dry ingredients. Work into a firm dough. Chill for at least 15 minutes. Roll out on a lightly floured board and use about two-thirds of the pastry to line the tin or plate. Put the rest aside.

To make the filling, chop the peel if in large pieces. Beat it into the cheese. Add the lemon rind and juice, and the sugar and mix in lightly. Beat the cream into the eggs and blend the liquid with the cheese mixture. Turn the mixture into the pastry case. Make long strips with the reserved pastry, and use them to make a criss-cross lattice pattern on the cheesecake. Seal the edges to the pastry rim with a little of the unused egg white. Brush some of the remaining egg white over the pastry strips. Bake at 200°C, 400°F, Gas 6, for 10 minutes, then reduce the heat to 180°C, 350°F, Gas 4, and bake for a further 30–35 minutes, or until the filling is just firm in the centre. Cool in the tin, and serve cold.

LINDY'S ORIGINAL CHEESECAKE

Serves 12–14

BASE
125g (4oz) flour
40g (1½oz) castor sugar
1 teaspoon grated lemon rind
¼ teaspoon vanilla essence
1 egg yolk
60g (2oz) butter

FILLING
1kg (2lb) low-fat soft cheese
250g (8oz) full-fat soft cheese
275g (9oz) castor sugar
30g (1oz) flour
1½ teaspoons grated orange rind
1½ teaspoons grated lemon rind
¼ teaspoon vanilla essence
5 eggs and 2 egg yolks
4 tablespoons double cream

Sift the flour into a bowl, add the sugar and lemon rind and mix. Make a well in the centre and add the essence, yolk and butter. Work together quickly to make a dough. Wrap in waxed paper and chill for 1 hour. Oil the base (without the sides) of a deep 22cm (8½ inch) loose-based or springform cake tin. Roll out the dough 3mm (⅛ inch) thick on a floured board. Lay part on the base, and trim off by running the rolling pin over the sharp edges. Bake at 200°C, 400°F, Gas 6, for 8–10 minutes or until firm and lightly coloured. Cool. Grease the sides of the tin and fit in place over the base. Roll out the unused pastry into a wide strip 3mm (⅛ inch) thick and use to line the sides of the tin.

To make the filling, beat the cheeses together until soft and well blended. Mix in the sugar, flour, orange and lemon rind and essence. Stir in the eggs and yolks lightly, one at a time. Stir in the cream. Turn into the pastry case. Bake at 240°C, 475°F, Gas 9, for 10 minutes. Reduce the heat to 110°C, 225°F, Gas ¼, and bake for 1 hour. Remove from the oven and cool in the tin, removing it just before serving. Eat within 12 hours.

Note This recipe was given to the author by Lindy's restaurant in New York, U.S.A. in 1962.

One-Stage Lemon Cottage Cheesecake

Serves 6–8

BASE
90g (3oz) margarine
175g (6oz) digestive biscuit crumbs
40g (1½oz) light soft brown sugar
½ teaspoon grated lemon rind

FILLING
4 eggs
175g (6oz) castor sugar
30g (1oz) flour
¼ teaspoon salt
2 tablespoons lemon juice
¼ teaspoon grated lemon rind
100ml (4floz) double cream
3×226g (8oz) cartons cottage cheese

Line the base and grease the inside of a 20cm (8 inch) loose-based or springform cake tin. Melt the margarine and work it into the crumbs and sugar with the lemon rind. Press the mixture evenly over the base and 2.5cm (1 inch) of the sides of the tin with the back of a spoon. Chill while making the filling.

Using an electric mixer if possible, beat the eggs until thick, gradually adding the sugar. Beat in the flour and salt. Strain the lemon juice and beat into the mixture with the lemon rind and cream. Sieve the cheese, then beat it in, and continue beating until the mixture is fully blended and smooth. Turn into the chilled tin. Bake at 170°C, 325°F, Gas 3, for 1 hour. Cool in the turned-off oven for another hour, then remove and allow to finish cooling in the tin. Run a sharp knife round the inside of the tin to loosen the cheesecake, then remove the tin. Refrigerate for at least 4 hours. Serve with fresh raspberries or strawberries in summer, or with well-drained, canned yellow peaches.

Warsaw Sultana Cheesecake

Serves 6–8

BASE
1×23cm (9 inch) puff pastry flan case,
baked blind (see page 12)

FILLING
3 eggs, separated
60g (2oz) castor sugar
2×226g (8oz) cartons cottage cheese
1 tablespoon cornflour
½ teaspoon vanilla essence
150ml (¼pint) soured cream
60g (2oz) sultanas

TOPPING
castor **or** icing sugar

Cool the pastry case if newly baked. Beat the egg yolks and sugar together until thick and pale. Sieve the cheese into a bowl, add the egg-sugar mixture and stir lightly. Separately, blend the cornflour with the vanilla essence and a little of the cream to make a smooth paste. Blend into the cheese mixture, then mix in the remaining cream and the sultanas. Whisk the egg whites until fairly stiff, stir 2 tablespoons into the cheese mixture, then fold in the rest. Pile the filling gently into the pastry case. Bake at 180°C, 350°F, Gas 4, for 55 minutes–1 hour, or until firm in the centre. Cool completely in the turned-off oven. Sprinkle sugar over the top and serve.

RICH NATURAL CHEESECAKE

Serves 10–12

BASE
90g (3oz) butter
150g (5oz) granary **or** wholemeal breadcrumbs
30g (1oz) ground almonds
60g (2oz) light muscovado sugar

FILLING
100g (3½oz) butter
2×226g (8oz) cartons cottage cheese
500g (1lb) full-fat soft cheese
250g (8oz) light muscovado sugar
4 eggs
5 tablespoons wholemeal flour
3 tablespoons arrowroot
¼ teaspoon ground cinnamon
2 tablespoons lemon juice
1½ teaspoons vanilla essence
300ml (½pint) soured cream

TOPPING
40g (1½oz) demerara sugar

Line the base and grease the inside of a 23cm (9 inch) loose-based cake tin about 7.5cm (3 inches) deep. Melt the butter and mix with the breadcrumbs, almonds and sugar. Press the mixture evenly all over the base of the tin. Chill while making the filling.

Melt the butter and allow to cool. Sieve the cottage cheese into a large bowl. Beat both cheeses together for 2 minutes. Still beating, add the sugar gradually, then the eggs, one at a time, followed by the flour, arrowroot, cinnamon, lemon juice and vanilla essence. Separately, mix together the cooled butter and the cream, and stir them into the cheese mixture. Pour the mixture into the tin, and bake for 1¾ hours at 170°C, 325°F, Gas 3. Cool in the turned-off oven for 2½ hours, then leave the door ajar until the cheesecake is cold. Refrigerate for 12–18 hours before use. Before serving, remove from the tin and sprinkle with the sugar.

This light, rich party cheesecake uses only organic ingredients.

UPSIDE-DOWN CHEESECAKE

Serves 6–8

BASE
3 tablespoons golden rusk crumbs

FILLING
5 eggs, separated
150g (5oz) castor sugar
2 tablespoons flour
1 tablespoon semolina
2×226g (8oz) cartons cottage cheese
100ml (4floz) soured cream
grated rind 1 lemon
1 teaspoon vanilla essence

Line the base of a 22cm (8½ inch) cake tin. Generously grease the inside with butter and sprinkle with the crumbs.

Beat the egg yolks and sugar together in a large bowl until very pale and thick. Sprinkle with the flour and semolina. Sieve the cheese and beat it in, followed by the cream, lemon rind and vanilla essence. Whisk the egg whites until they hold soft peaks and fold them in. Turn the mixture gently into the prepared tin. Bake at 180°C, 350°F, Gas 4, for 1–1¼ hours, until well risen and just firm in the centre. Cool in the turned-off oven for 30 minutes. Take out and run a sharp knife round the edge of the cheesecake, then leave to cool completely. Invert the cooled cake on to a serving plate. Lift off the tin, and peel off the lining paper carefully. The cake will have brownish sides and a peach-coloured top.

Rich Natural Cheesecake

CHOCOLATE SULTANA CHEESECAKE

Serves 6–8

BASE
125g (4oz) flour
salt
60g (2oz) butter
30g (1oz) castor sugar
1 egg yolk
1½ teaspoons water

FILLING
2 eggs
90g (3oz) castor sugar
250g (8oz) home-made,
unsalted yogurt cheese (see page 9)
2 tablespoons single cream
grated rind and juice 1 lemon
60g (2oz) flour
60g (2oz) sultanas
90g (3oz) plain dark chocolate
1 egg white

TOPPING
30g (1oz) icing sugar
150ml (¼pint) natural yogurt
chocolate curls (see page 14)

Line the base and lightly grease the inside of a 20cm (8 inch) loose-based cake tin. Sift the flour and a pinch of salt into a bowl. Rub in the butter with the fingertips until the mixture resembles fine crumbs. Mix in the sugar. Separately, blend the egg yolk with the water. Add to the dry ingredients and work to a smooth, firm dough. Chill for 1 hour, then roll out on a lightly floured board into a 20cm (8 inch) round. Press the pastry round into the base of the cake tin. Chill while making the filling.

Whisk the eggs and sugar together until light and thick. Separately, beat together the cheese and cream. Strain the lemon juice, and beat it into the cheese mixture with the lemon rind. Combine lightly with the egg-sugar mixture, then fold in the flour and sultanas. Melt the chocolate in a bowl over a pan of simmering water. When melted stir into the main mixture, blending completely. Whisk the egg white until stiff and fold in gently. Turn the mixture on to the chilled pastry base, and bake at 190°C, 375°F, Gas 5, for 45 minutes–1 hour, or until the filling is just firm.

While baking, stir the icing sugar very gently into the yogurt so as not to liquefy it. When the cheesecake is baked, spoon the sugar-yogurt mixture over the top. Raise the oven heat to 220°C, 425°F, Gas 7, return the cheesecake to the oven and bake for 5–10 minutes until the topping is set. Take out, and cool completely in the tin. Chill for 1–1½ hours. Decorate with chocolate curls (see page 14) just before serving.

LUXEMBURG KAES KUCH

Serves 6

BASE
250g (8oz) flour
2 teaspoons baking powder
¼ teaspoon salt
1 tablespoon castor sugar
125g (4oz) butter
175–200ml (5–6floz) milk

FILLING
500g (1lb) unsalted home-made milk curd
cheese (see page 9 and **Note** below)
3 eggs, separated
100ml (4floz) double cream
grated rind and juice ½ lemon
125g (4oz) castor sugar
¼ teaspoon salt

Grease the inside of an 18cm (7 inch) loose-based sandwich cake tin. Sift the flour, baking powder and salt for the base into a bowl. Mix in the sugar. Rub in the butter lightly. Mix to a springy dough with the milk. Roll out or pat the dough into the right shape to line the tin.

To make the filling, beat the cheese until smooth. Beat in the egg yolks, one at a time. Then stir in the cream, lemon rind and juice. Lastly, mix in 90g (3oz) of the sugar, putting the rest aside. Mix well. Turn into the pastry case and bake at 190°C, 375°F, Gas 5, for 35 minutes or until the cheesecake is just firm.

Shortly before the end of the cooking time whisk the egg whites and salt together until stiff, adding half of the remaining sugar. Continue whisking until the meringue is stiff and glossy. Fold in the last of the sugar. Reduce the oven heat to 150°C, 300°F, Gas 2. Remove the cheesecake and pile the meringue on top, taking care to cover the filling mixture completely. Return to the oven and bake until the meringue is set and lightly browned. Remove from the tin and serve warm or cool.

Note Unsalted soft curd cheese is available from health food stores if you do not make your own.

HEREFORD CURD CAKE

Serves 2–3

BASE
90g (3oz) shortcrust pastry (see page 12)

FILLING
60g (2oz) butter
200g (7oz) slightly salted home-made milk curd cheese
(see page 9) **or** cottage cheese
1 large egg
2 teaspoons light rum
30g (1oz) castor sugar
grated rind 1 small lemon
salt
1 tablespoon currants

TOPPING
1 teaspoon butter
grated nutmeg

Grease a deep 15cm (6 inch) patty tin or pie plate. Roll out the pastry on a lightly floured board and use to line the tin.

Soften the butter and place in a large bowl. Sieve the cheese into the bowl and beat in the egg, followed by the rum, sugar, lemon rind, a pinch of salt and the currants. Turn the mixture into the pastry case. For the topping, soften the butter. Sprinkle the top of the filling with the nutmeg and dot with the butter. Bake at 190°C, 375°F, Gas 5, for 35 minutes or until the filling is just firm in the centre, and the surface is lightly browned. Cool in the tin. Serve just warm or cold, as a dessert, with apple jelly or stewed apples.

Note This cheesecake stays moist. Do not freeze.

THREE-CHEESE HONEY CHEESECAKE

Serves 10

BASE
250g (8oz) wholemeal flour
2 eggs
4 tablespoons clear honey
60g (2oz) margarine

FILLING
1×225g (8oz) packet Philadelphia soft cheese
125g (4oz) clear honey
60g (2oz) margarine
2 eggs, separated
2×226g (8oz) cartons cottage cheese
60g (2oz) Gruyère cheese
1 teaspoon grated nutmeg
grated rind and juice 1 lemon

TOPPING
Gruyère cheese to decorate

Line the base and grease the inside of a 20cm (8 inch) loose-based cake tin. Sift the flour into a bowl, make a hollow in the centre, and put in the eggs, honey and margarine. Work them into the flour to make a soft, pasty dough. With the back of a spoon, press it evenly all over the base and sides of the tin. Chill while making the filling.

Bring the Philadelphia cheese up to room temperature. Beat together the honey, margarine and egg yolks until fully blended. Sieve in the cottage and Philadelphia cheeses, grate in the Gruyère cheese, and mix in the nutmeg, lemon rind and juice. Whisk the egg whites until fairly stiff. Stir 1 tablespoonful into the cheese mixture, then fold in the rest. Turn the mixture into the chilled case. Bake at 180°C, 350°F, Gas 4, for 50 minutes–1 hour, or until the filling is just firm and light gold. Cool in the turned-off oven with the door ajar until fully cooled, then chill for a further 12 hours at least. Before serving, grate enough cheese to make about 3 tablespoons and sprinkle over the top of the cheesecake.

MILK CURD CHEESECAKE

Serves 4–6

BASE
60g (2oz) digestive biscuit crumbs
2 teaspoons castor sugar
30g (1oz) butter

FILLING
125g (4oz) home-made milk curd cheese
(see page 9)
60g (2oz) butter
grated rind and juice ½ lemon
1 teaspoon orange juice
2 eggs, separated
60g (2oz) ground almonds
60g (2oz) castor sugar
2 tablespoons self-raising flour

This cheesecake is prepared and baked upside down, and inverted just before serving.

Line the base and grease with butter the inside of an 18cm (7 inch) sandwich cake tin. Put the cheese in a bowl and break it up with a fork. Melt the butter without letting it get hot. Strain the lemon and orange juice together. Stir the butter, lemon rind, fruit juices and egg yolks into the cheese, followed by the almonds and sugar. Beat the mixture until well blended. Sift the flour and fold into the mixture. Whisk the egg whites until stiff but not dry, and fold in lightly. Turn the mixture into the prepared tin.

Mix the crumbs with the sugar. Melt the butter and combine with the dry ingredients to make a crumbly mixture. Scatter it lightly and evenly over the filling. Bake at 220°C, 425°F, Gas 7, for 10 minutes, then reduce the heat to 180°C, 350°F, Gas 4, and bake for another 20 minutes, or until the cheesecake is firm and dry in the centre when pierced with a thin skewer. Cover loosely with greaseproof paper if the crumbs begin to over-brown while baking.

Loosen the cheesecake from the sides of the tin with a flexible spatula or palette knife, then leave to cool in the tin. Invert gently on to a serving plate so that the crumbs form the base. Peel off the lining paper. Serve cut in wedges.

ALPINE CHEESECAKE

Serves 6–8

BASE
1×20cm (8 inch) pastry flan case,
baked blind (see page 12)

FILLING
175g (6oz) Gruyère cheese
30g (1oz) self-raising flour
90g (3oz) castor sugar
grated rind and juice 1 lemon
1 egg yolk
5 tablespoons natural yogurt
2 egg whites

Any type of pastry is suitable for this cheesecake. Grate the cheese into a large bowl, add the flour, sugar and lemon rind, and mix thoroughly. Separately, beat the egg yolk lightly, then stir it gently into the yogurt. Strain the lemon juice and stir into the egg-yogurt mixture. Mix gently but thoroughly with the dry ingredients. Whisk the egg whites until stiff but not dry. Stir 1 tablespoon into the cheese mixture, then fold in the rest. Turn the mixture gently into the pastry case set on a heavy baking sheet. Bake at 170°C, 325°F, Gas 3, for 35–45 minutes, or until firm in the centre. Cool in the turned-off oven with the door ajar for 10–15 minutes, then finish cooling on a wire rack. Serve cold.

CHEDDAR CHEESECAKE

Serves 6–8

BASE
1×20cm (8 inch) shortcrust pastry
flan case, baked blind (see page 12)

FILLING
175g (6oz) mild Cheddar cheese
grated rind and juice 1 lemon
30g (1oz) self-raising flour
90g (3oz) castor sugar
1 egg, separated
5 tablespoons natural yogurt
1 egg white

Grate the cheese into a large bowl, add the lemon rind, flour and sugar and mix thoroughly. Separately, beat the egg yolk lightly and gently stir in the yogurt. Strain and stir in the lemon juice. Mix the liquid into the dry ingredients little by little, to make a smooth mixture. Whisk both egg whites together until fairly stiff. Stir 1 tablespoon into the cheese mixture, then fold in the rest lightly but thoroughly. Turn gently into the flan case set on a baking sheet. Bake at 170°C, 325°F, Gas 3, for 35–45 minutes or until firm in the centre and lightly browned. Cool on the baking sheet. Serve cold.

UNBAKED CHEESECAKES

BANANA AND CHOCOLATE CHEESECAKE

Serves 8–11

BASE
30g (1oz) milk chocolate
60g (2oz) butter
125g (4oz) chocolate-coated digestive biscuit crumbs

FILLING
4 tablespoons cold water
1 packet (15g/½oz) gelatine
250g (8oz) full-fat soft cheese
90g (3oz) castor sugar
2 eggs, separated
150ml (¼pint) natural **or** lemon-flavoured yogurt
grated rind and juice ½ lemon
150ml (¼pint) whipping cream
2 firm, ripe bananas

TOPPING
grated milk chocolate **or** chocolate curls
(see page 14) to decorate

Grease the inside of a 20cm (8 inch) loose-based cake tin. Melt the chocolate and butter on a plate over a pan of simmering water, and mix thoroughly with the crumbs. Press in an even layer all over the base of the tin. Chill while making the filling.

Put the water in a small, heatproof bowl. Sprinkle on the gelatine and allow to soften. Then stand the bowl in a pan of very hot water and stir until the gelatine dissolves. Keep aside. Beat the cheese with the sugar until soft and creamy. Beat in the egg yolks, followed by the yogurt, lemon rind and juice. Stir in the gelatine, taking care not to let lumps form. Working quickly, whip the cream until it just holds soft peaks and stir into the cheese mixture. Whisk the egg whites until fairly stiff, and fold them in. Slice the bananas, and put them in a single layer on the chilled base. Cover the cheesecake mixture and chill until set. Remove the tin, and decorate the top with grated chocolate or chocolate curls before serving.

Do not freeze this cheesecake.

BLACKCURRANT SKIM CHEESECAKE

Serves 4–6

BASE
30g (1oz) butter
1 tablespoon golden syrup
150g (5oz) digestive biscuit crumbs

FILLING
3 eggs, separated
300ml (½ pint) skimmed milk **or**
dried skimmed milk powder made up with water
30g (1oz) castor sugar
2 tablespoons cold water
1 packet (15g/½oz) gelatine
250g (8oz) cream cheese **or**
full-fat soft cheese
½ teaspoon grated lemon rind
1 tablespoon lemon juice

TOPPING
250g (8oz) fresh blackcurrants
4 tablespoons+2 teaspoons cold water
30g (1oz) castor sugar
2 teaspoons arrowroot

Line and grease the inside of a loose-based 15cm (6 inch) square, or an 18cm (7 inch) round cake tin. Melt the butter and syrup together gently. Cool slightly. Mix the crumbs with the butter and syrup. Press evenly all over the base of the cake tin. Chill while making the filling.

Whisk the egg yolks with a fork until liquid. Mix with the skimmed milk in a saucepan, and heat gently, stirring continuously, until the custard thickens. Remove from the heat and stir in the sugar. Leave to cool. Whisk the egg whites until stiff and put aside. Put the water in a small heatproof bowl. Sprinkle on the gelatine and allow to soften. Then stand the bowl in a pan of very hot water, and stir until the gelatine dissolves. Mash the cheese with a fork to soften it, gradually trickling in the gelatine, custard and the lemon rind. Strain the lemon juice and mix in. Whisk the mixture until it begins to thicken, then fold in the whisked egg whites lightly. Spoon the mixture over the chilled crumb base and leave in a cool place to set.

To make the topping, first top and tail the blackcurrants. Then put them in a saucepan with the 4 tablespoons water and sugar. Bring gently to the boil, and cook for 2 minutes. Strain the juice into a clean pan and keep the fruit aside. Blend the arrowroot to a cream with the 2 tablespoons cold water and stir into the juice. Heat gently, stirring, until the mixture clears and thickens. Add the fruit. Cool, covered.

Remove the cheesecake from the tin and peel off the lining paper. Place on a serving dish and spoon the blackcurrant sauce over. Serve at once, with whipped cream.

BLACK FOREST CHEESECAKE

Serves 8—10

BASE
90g (3oz) plain chocolate
75g (2½oz) butter
275g (9oz) plain chocolate digestive biscuit crumbs

FILLING AND TOPPING
1×425g (15oz) can pitted black cherries in syrup
350g (12oz) full-fat soft cheese
90g (3oz) castor sugar
2 eggs, separated
1 tablespoon kirsch
2 tablespoons cold water
1 packet (15g/½oz) gelatine
300ml (½ pint) double cream
1 tablespoon arrowroot
kirsch **or** lemon juice to taste
chocolate curls (see page 14)

Line and grease the base of a 23cm (9 inch) loose-based cake tin. Melt the chocolate and butter for the base together and mix with the crumbs. Press the mixture evenly all over the base of the tin and chill.

Drain the cherries, reserving the syrup, and cut them in half. Spread about one-third of the fruit on the chilled base and keep the rest aside. Cream the cheese and sugar together thoroughly, then beat in the egg yolks and kirsch. Put the water in a small heatproof bowl, sprinkle on the gelatine and allow to soften. Then stand the bowl in a pan of very hot water and stir until the gelatine dissolves. Leave to cool slightly while you beat the cream until it just holds soft peaks, and whisk the egg whites until stiff. Beat the gelatine into the cheese mixture little by little, taking care not to let lumps form, then fold in the cream, and finally the egg whites. Turn gently on to the base and chill until firm.

Make a cherry sauce. Blend the arrowroot to a cream with a little of the reserved syrup. Put the rest in a pan, add kirsch or lemon juice to taste, and bring just to boiling point. Stir in the arrowroot cream and continue stirring until the liquid thickens and clears. Use hot, or cool under damped paper for use cold.

Remove the tin from the cheesecake. Just before serving, decorate the top with the remaining cherries. Spoon a little cherry sauce over the cherries, and arrange the chocolate curls around the edge. Serve the remaining cherry sauce separately.

The cheesecake can be frozen before decoration.

Black Forest Cheesecake

AS-YOU-LIKE-IT CHEESECAKE

Serves 4–6

BASE
125g (4oz) digestive biscuit crumbs
30g (1oz) castor sugar
40g (1½oz) butter

FILLING AND TOPPING
grated rind and juice 1 lemon
4 tablespoons cold water
1 packet (15g/½oz) gelatine
250g (8oz) full-fat soft cheese
90g (3oz) castor sugar
2 eggs, separated
150ml (¼pint) soured cream
1 tablespoon sugar

Line and grease the base of an 18cm (7 inch) loose-based cake tin. Mix the crumbs and sugar in a bowl. Melt the butter, and mix it in. Press the mixture over the base of the tin. Chill while making the filling.

Put the lemon juice and water in a small heatproof bowl. Sprinkle on the gelatine and allow to soften. Then stand the bowl in a pan of very hot water, and stir until the gelatine dissolves. Cool to tepid. While cooling, beat the cheese until soft; beat in the castor sugar, then the egg yolks, one at a time. Stir in the cream. Stir in the gelatine slowly, to prevent lumps forming. Leave until almost set. Whisk the egg whites until stiff, and fold into the mixture. Turn it gently on to the base, and chill until set. Remove from the tin and sprinkle with the lemon rind and sugar just before serving. Top with rosettes of whipped cream if desired.

RICH CIDER CHEESECAKE

Serves 6–8

BASE
60g (2oz) butter
150g (5oz) digestive biscuit crumbs

FILLING
150ml (¼pint) medium-sweet cider
2 tablespoons cold water
1 packet (15g/½oz) gelatine
2 small eggs, separated
60g (2oz) castor sugar
350g (12oz) full-fat soft cheese
200ml (6fl oz) double cream

Line and grease the base of a 20cm (8 inch) loose-based cake tin. Melt the butter and mix well with the crumbs. Press evenly all over the base of the tin. Chill while making the filling.

Bring the cider to the boil in a saucepan, and reduce to 80ml (3 fl oz). Remove from the heat. Put the water in a small container, sprinkle on the gelatine, and allow to soften. Then add it to the hot cider and stir until it dissolves. Cool to tepid. In a large bowl, beat the egg yolks and sugar together until very pale and thick. Beat in the cheese in small portions until very smooth. Whip the cream to the same consistency as the cheese mixture and beat it in. Stir or beat in the cider and gelatine, taking care not to let lumps form. Whisk the egg whites until stiff and fold into the mixture. Turn gently on to the chilled base and chill again until set.

To serve, run a sharp knife round the inside of the cake tin, and lift out the cheesecake and base. Slide the cheesecake from the base on to a serving plate and serve with blackcurrant purée (see page 15) as a sauce.

GRAPEFRUIT CHEESECAKE BARS

Serves 8

BASE
90g (3oz) butter
175g (6oz) digestive biscuit crumbs
1 teaspoon grated lemon rind

FILLING
250g (8oz) full-fat soft cheese
1 teaspoon grated lemon rind
2 grapefruits
1×397g (14oz) can sweetened condensed milk
3–4 tablespoons lemon juice

Cut a piece of bakewell paper which will fit the base of an 18×28cm (7×11 inch) baking tin at least 4cm (1½ inches) deep and overhang on opposite sides. Line the tin with it. Grease the uncovered sides lightly. Melt the butter and work in the crumbs and lemon rind. Press the mixture evenly all over the base of the tin. Chill while making the filling.

Beat the cheese until soft, adding the lemon rind. Remove all skin, pith and pips from the grapefruits over a soup plate, to catch any juice. Chop the flesh into small bits, and keep aside. Little by little, beat the condensed milk, grapefruit juice and lemon juice into the cheese (use only 3 tablespoons lemon juice if the grapefruits are very juicy). Fold in the bits of fruit. Turn the mixture on to the chilled base, and chill again for 4 hours or until firmly set. Cut into bars for serving.

Note For easy cutting, remove the cheesecake from the tin first, by lifting the two overhanging edges of bakewell paper.

PLUM PIE CHEESECAKE

Serves 4—6

BASE
1×18cm (7 inch) pastry flan case, baked blind, (see page 12)

FILLING
200g (7oz) plum pie filling
250g (8oz) full-fat soft cheese
150ml (¼pint) double cream
1 teaspoon lemon juice
30g (1oz) castor sugar

Use the pastry of your choice for the flan case. Sieve the pie filling. Put the cheese and cream into a bowl, and beat them together until thick and smooth. Beat in the lemon juice and sugar. Then beat in 2–3 tablespoons pie filling. Taste, and add any extra pie filling needed to give the flavour and consistency you want, putting the remaining pie filling aside. Beat again until the mixture is smooth, then pile it into the flan case. Chill well. Spoon pie filling round the edge of the cheesecake to decorate.

LEMON AND REDCURRANT CHEESECAKE

Serves 6–8

BASE
90g (3oz) butter
3 tablespoons golden syrup
175g (6oz) 30% bran flake crumbs

FILLING
2 eggs, separated
60g (2oz) castor sugar
250g (8oz) full-fat soft cheese
3 tablespoons lemon juice
2 tablespoons cold water
1 packet (15g/½oz) gelatine
150ml (¼pint) double **or** whipping cream

TOPPING
4 tablespoons redcurrant jelly
2 tablespoons warm water
125g (4oz) fresh redcurrants and
castor sugar as required (optional)

All the ingredients should be at room temperature. Line and grease the base and sides of a 22cm (8½ inch) loose-based sandwich cake tin. Melt the butter and syrup together in a medium-sized saucepan, and stir in the crumbs until well coated all over. Press the crumbs over the base and sides of the tin to form a shell. Trim the top and brush off any loose crumbs as described on page 14. Bake for 10 minutes at 180°C, 350°F, Gas 4. Remove from the oven and cool completely.

Cream the egg yolks and sugar thoroughly. Sieve the cheese and beat it in slowly, until very smooth. Trickle in the lemon juice, and beat until fully blended in. Put the water in a small heatproof bowl, sprinkle on the gelatine and allow to soften. Then stand the bowl in a pan of very hot water, and stir until the gelatine dissolves. Cool to tepid. Whip the cream until semi-stiff, and whisk the egg whites until they form soft peaks. Mix the tepid gelatine into the cheese mixture thoroughly. When it thickens and is almost at setting point, fold in the cream and then the egg whites quickly and lightly, blending completely in each case. Turn the mixture into the cooled shell, and smooth the top level. Leave until fully set.

To make the topping, melt the redcurrant jelly with the water, and leave until almost cold but not yet reset. If you wish, add sweetened fresh redcurrants to the topping. Spoon it lightly over the filling and leave to set. Run a sharp knife round the inside of the tin to loosen the case. Remove the cheesecake, and slide it on to a serving plate. Serve cut in wedges.

Lemon and Redcurrant Cheesecake

CHOCOLATE AND LEMON CURL CHEESECAKE

Serves 6

BASE
125g (4oz) butter
2 tablespoons clear honey
200g (7oz) digestive biscuit crumbs
60g (2oz) plain chocolate

FILLING
250g (8oz) full-fat soft cheese
juice ½ lemon
1 egg, separated
2 tablespoons clear honey
150ml (¼ pint) cold milk
vanilla essence
2 teaspoons brandy (optional)
2 tablespoons cold water
1 packet (15g/½oz) gelatine

TOPPING
½ lemon
30g (1oz) plain chocolate

Line the base and grease the inside of a 20cm (8 inch) loose-based sandwich cake tin, or a flan ring set on a baking sheet. Melt the butter and honey for the base, and work in the crumbs. Press the mixture evenly all over the base and sides of the tin or ring. Trim the top, and brush off any loose crumbs as described on page 14. Break up the chocolate for the base, and melt it on a plate over a pan of simmering water. Spread it evenly all over the base of the case. Chill while making the filling.

Soften the cheese well with the back of a spoon, working in the lemon juice. Separately, beat the egg yolk, honey and milk together in a heatproof bowl until blended. Stand the bowl in a pan of simmering water, and beat until the custard thickens. Cool for 2 minutes, then beat it into the cheese little by little, with a few drops of vanilla essence and the brandy if used. Put the water in another heatproof bowl, sprinkle on the gelatine and allow to soften. Then stand the bowl in a pan of very hot water and stir until the gelatine dissolves. Cool for 2–3 minutes, then stir lightly but thoroughly into the cheese mixture, taking care not to let lumps of jelly form. Leave until almost at setting point.

Whisk the egg white until it holds soft peaks, and fold into the cheese mixture. Turn the mixture quickly into the chilled case, and chill again until set.

While setting, slice the ½ lemon. Then cut each slice from the centre to the edge, and twist it to form a curl. Melt the chocolate for the topping on a plate over a pan of simmering water. Just before serving, arrange the lemon curls on the cheesecake, and pipe on lines of chocolate to decorate it.

BRAN FLAKE DESSERT CHEESECAKE

Serves 4–6

BASE
175g (6oz) 30% bran flakes
90g (3oz) butter
3 tablespoons clear honey

FILLING
2 eggs, separated
60g (2oz) castor sugar
250g (8oz) full-fat soft cheese
4 tablespoons lemon juice
2 tablespoons cold water
1 packet (15g/½oz) gelatine
150ml (¼pint) double cream
grated rind ½ lemon

Grease the inside of a 20cm (8 inch) flan ring on a baking sheet. Grease the baking sheet lightly too. Crush the flakes lightly between 2 sheets of paper with a rolling pin. Melt the butter and honey together in a medium-sized saucepan, and mix in the flakes thoroughly until well coated. Press the flakes firmly into the flan ring to form a shell. Trim the top, and brush off any loose crumbs as described on page 14. Bake at 180°C, 350°F, Gas 4, for 10 minutes. Cool completely.

To make the filling, cream the egg yolks and sugar together until thick and light. Beat in the cheese slowly until completely smooth. Add the lemon juice and beat until very smooth. Put the water in a small, heatproof bowl, sprinkle on the gelatine and allow to soften. Then stand the bowl in a pan of hot water and stir until the gelatine dissolves. Whip the cream until semi-stiff. Whisk the egg whites until they hold soft peaks. Mix the cream and lemon rind into the cheese mixture, then stir in the dissolved gelatine gradually to prevent lumps forming. Fold in the egg whites lightly but thoroughly, and leave to thicken. When the mixture is thickening and almost at setting point, pile it into the flan ring case. Leave in a cool place until fully set. Remove the flan ring, slide the cheesecake on to a serving plate, and serve cut in wedges.

LOGANBERRY CHEESECAKE

Serves 6

BASE
60g (2oz) butter
125g (4oz) any plain biscuit crumbs

FILLING AND TOPPING
1 × 410g (14½oz) can loganberries in syrup
1 packet (15g/½oz) gelatine
125g (4oz) full-fat soft cheese
4 tablespoons dried skimmed milk powder
made up to 300ml (½pint) with water
1 tablespoon lemon juice
1 tablespoon kirsch
60g (2oz) castor sugar
5 tablespoons whipping cream
1 teaspoon arrowroot
½ teaspoon extra kirsch (optional)

Line and grease the base of an 18cm (7 inch) loose-based cake tin. Soften the butter and mix with the crumbs thoroughly. Press evenly all over the base of the tin. Chill while making the filling.

Drain the fruit, reserving 12 loganberries for the topping, and the syrup. Sieve the rest of the fruit to make a smooth purée. Put 2 tablespoons of the reserved syrup in a small heatproof bowl, sprinkle on the gelatine and allow to soften. Stand the bowl in a pan of very hot water and stir until the gelatine dissolves. Cool to tepid.

Soften the cheese and mix smoothly with the milk. Mix in the lemon juice, kirsch, and sugar. Stir in the loganberry purée lightly. Whip and fold in the cream. Mix in the gelatine slowly but thoroughly, without letting lumps form. Turn the mixture on to the chilled base, level the top and chill again until set.

To make the topping, measure out 150ml (¼ pint) of the reserved syrup. Blend a little of the measured quantity with the arrowroot to make a smooth cream. Bring the rest to the boil in a small saucepan. Blend in the arrowroot cream, and simmer until the syrup thickens and clears. Remove the pan from the heat and gently mix in the reserved fruit and the extra kirsch if used. Cool, covered. When ready to serve, remove the cheesecake from the tin, and spoon the cooled syrup over it.

SUMMER ORANGE CHEESECAKE

Serves 12

BASE
200g (7oz) butter
350g (12oz) Rich Tea **or** similar biscuit crumbs
125g (4oz) castor sugar

FILLING
4 large oranges
$\frac{3}{4}$ lemon jelly tablet to set 400ml ($\frac{3}{4}$ pint) liquid
150ml ($\frac{1}{4}$ pint) very hot water
500g (1lb) full-fat soft cheese
125g (4oz) castor sugar

TOPPING
$\frac{1}{4}$ lemon jelly tablet to set 150ml ($\frac{1}{4}$ pint) liquid
4 tablespoons very hot water
juice 1 orange
3 oranges
1 × 227g (8oz) jar fine shred orange marmalade

Lightly grease the inside of a 25cm (10 inch) flan ring and place it on a flat serving plate. Soften the butter and work the crumbs and sugar into it until well blended. Press the mixture evenly all over the base and sides of the flan ring. Trim the top and brush off any loose crumbs as described on page 14. Chill.

To make the filling grate the rind from 1 of the oranges, and squeeze the juice of all 4. Chop the $\frac{3}{4}$ jelly tablet and put it in a basin with the water. Stir until the jelly dissolves, then add the orange juice and cool to tepid. Beat the cheese until soft with the sugar and orange rind. Trickle in the tepid jelly, beating all the time to prevent lumps forming. Spoon the filling into the chilled case, and chill again until set.

While chilling, make the topping. Chop the $\frac{1}{4}$ jelly tablet and put it in a basin with the water. Stir until dissolved. Add the orange juice, and chill until firmly set. Cut the flesh of the oranges for decorating free of all skin, pith and pips. Arrange the segments of flesh around the edge of the cheesecake. Warm the marmalade just enough to make it liquid, brush it over the cheesecake and chill. Chop the clear orange jelly and heap it in the centre of the cheesecake. Remove the flan ring and serve.

NESSELRODE CHEESECAKE

Serves 4–6

BASE
75g (2$\frac{1}{2}$oz) butter
150g (5oz) Marie biscuit crumbs

FILLING AND TOPPING
90g (3oz) glacé cherries
60g (2oz) chopped mixed peel
250g (8oz) full-fat soft cheese
2 tablespoons clear honey
175g (6oz) unsweetened, canned chestnut purée
200ml (6fl oz) whipping cream
1 tablespoon light rum
2 tablespoons cold water
1 packet (15g/$\frac{1}{2}$oz) gelatine

Line and grease the base of a deep 15cm (6 inch) loose-based cake tin. Melt the butter and stir in the crumbs. Press them evenly over the base of the prepared tin. Chill.

Put 3 glacé cherries aside for decoration. Rinse the rest in hot water, pat dry and chop finely. Mix with the peel and put aside.

Sieve the cheese and mix in the honey, blending thoroughly. Sieve the chestnut purée if stiff. Whip the cream until semi-stiff, and mix it with the chestnut purée and rum until smooth and well blended. Fold the cheese and chestnut mixtures together. Put the water in a small heatproof bowl, sprinkle on the gelatine and allow to soften. Then stand the bowl in a pan of very hot water and stir until the gelatine dissolves. Allow to cool. Stir into the cheese mixture gradually to prevent lumps forming. Chill the mixture until thick and almost at setting point.

Assemble the dessert as follows. Spoon an even layer of cheese mixture over the chilled base. Sprinkle well with the cherry-peel mixture. Working quickly, repeat the layers until both mixtures are used, finishing with a layer of cheese mixture. Smooth the top level or make a swirled pattern. Cover loosely, and chill until fully set and firm, then remove the tin. Halve the remaining cherries and use to decorate before serving.

Summer Orange Cheesecake

HIGHLAND CHEESECAKE

Serves 4

BASE
40g (1½oz) butter
90g (3oz) plain oatcake crumbs
30g (1oz) dark soft brown sugar

FILLING AND TOPPING
orange jelly tablet to set 600ml (1 pint) liquid
Drambuie liqueur to taste (optional)
150ml (¼ pint) boiling water
2 tablespoons orange jelly marmalade
250g (8oz) full-fat soft cheese
60g (2oz) castor sugar
grated rind 1 orange
150ml (¼ pint) orange juice
golden oatmeal topping (see page 14)

Line and grease the base of a 15cm (6 inch) loose-based cake tin. Melt the butter, and mix in the crumbs and sugar. Press the mixture evenly all over the base of the tin. Chill while making the filling.

Put half the jelly tablet aside. Chop the remaining ½ jelly tablet. Substitute 1–2 tablespoons Drambuie for an equal quantity of boiling water if you wish. Pour the hot liquid over the chopped jelly, and stir until dissolved. Leave to cool until beginning to thicken. While cooling, spread the marmalade thinly over the chilled base. Beat the cheese until soft, and beat in the sugar and orange rind.

When the jelly is approaching setting point, mix it lightly, little by little, into the cheese, taking care not to let lumps form. Turn the mixture on to the chilled base, and chill again until set.

Put the reserved ½ jelly tablet in a heatproof bowl, and make jelly for the topping with the orange juice in the same way as for the filling mixture, substituting 1–2 tablespoons Drambuie for an equal quantity of orange juice if you wish. Cool. Just before it reaches setting point, pour a few spoonfuls at a time over the filling, and rotate the tin to spread the jelly evenly. Chill for at least 30 minutes. Remove from the tin and sprinkle with one third the recipe quantity of golden oatmeal topping (see page 14) just before serving.

MOCHA CHEESECAKE

Serves 8

BASE
75g (2½oz) butter
60g (2oz) milk chocolate
30g (1oz) castor sugar
125g (4oz) milk chocolate digestive biscuit crumbs

FILLING
1 tablespoon cocoa powder
300ml (½ pint) cold black coffee
1½ packets (25g/¾oz) gelatine
500g (1 lb) full-fat soft cheese
125g (4oz) castor sugar
5 tablespoons – 150ml (¼ pint) whipping cream

TOPPING
2–3 tablespoons grated milk chocolate
milk chocolate curls **or** caraque (see page 14)

Line and grease the base of a 20cm (8 inch) loose-based cake tin. Soften the butter and melt the chocolate on a plate over a pan of simmering water. Work the chocolate into the butter with the sugar and crumbs. Press the mixture evenly all over the base of the tin.

Mix the cocoa powder to a smooth cream with a little of the coffee. Put the rest of the coffee in a heatproof bowl, sprinkle on the gelatine and allow to soften. Blend in the cocoa cream, then stand the bowl in a pan of very hot water and stir until the gelatine dissolves. Cool to tepid. While cooling, beat the cheese and sugar together until creamy. Trickle in the cooled gelatine mixture, beating all the time to prevent lumps of jelly forming. Whip the cream separately and whisk into the cheese mixture. Turn on to the chilled base, and chill again until set.

When the cheesecake is set remove from the tin. Decorate the sides with grated chocolate and the top with chocolate curls or caraque before serving.

CHERRY CHARLOTTE CHEESECAKE

Serves 4–6

BASE
2 tablespoons red cherry jam
24 boudoir **or** sponge finger biscuits

FILLING
250g (8oz) fresh **or** canned morello cherries
water as required
lemon juice as required
clear honey as required
1 packet (15g/$\frac{1}{2}$oz) gelatine
250g (8oz) low-fat soft cheese
150ml ($\frac{1}{4}$pint) soured cream
2 egg whites

TOPPING
whipped cream and red cherry jam to decorate

Using bakewell paper, line the base and sides of a 15cm (6 inch) loose-based or springform cake tin. Sieve the jam. Place biscuits round the sides of the tin, set on end, with the sugared or rounded sides outward. Use the jam to stick the long edges of the biscuits together so that there are no gaps between them. Trim the projecting tops of the biscuits level with the rim of the tin. Keep the trimmed-off pieces and remaining whole biscuits aside.

If fresh fruit is used, first remove the stalks. Then simmer the cherries in a very little water, a few drops of lemon juice if required, and honey to taste, until they are soft. Remove the stones and drain, reserving the syrup. If canned cherries are used, simmer them in their own syrup with the same flavourings. Stone if necessary and drain, reserving the syrup. Allow the fruit to cool.

Place 3 tablespoons of the reserved syrup in a small heatproof bowl. Sprinkle on the gelatine and allow to soften. Then stand the bowl in a pan of very hot water, and stir until the gelatine dissolves. Cool until tepid. While cooling, beat the cheese until soft and creamy, and mix in the cream. Separately, whisk the egg whites until stiff but not dry.

Mix the cooled gelatine into the cheese-cream mixture, stirring well to prevent any lumps forming. Chill until just beginning to thicken. Fold in the fruit, then the egg whites. Spoon the mixture gently into the sponge biscuit case, and level the top. Cover with a flat layer of the reserved biscuits and biscuit pieces. Chill for 2–3 hours.

Invert the tin on to a serving plate. Remove the tin, and gently peel off the bakewell paper. Decorate the top of the cheesecake with alternate rosettes of piped whipped cream and blobs of red jam.

CASSATA CHEESECAKE

Serves 10

CAKE LAYERS
3 eggs, separated
40g (1½oz) castor sugar
2 teaspoons orange juice
1 teaspoon grated orange rind
salt
30g (1oz) flour

FILLING
750g (1½lb) low-fat soft cheese
75g (2½oz) castor sugar
100ml (4 floz) double cream
60g (2oz) glacé fruits (cherries, pineapple, etc)
60g (2oz) plain chocolate (optional)

COVERING
300ml (½pint) whipping cream
60g (2oz) icing sugar
glacé fruit to decorate (optional)

Line and grease the base and sides of a 33×23cm (13×9 inch) Swiss roll tin. Beat together the egg yolks and sugar until thick and pale. Beat in the orange juice and rind. Separately, whisk the egg whites and a pinch of salt until stiff. Fold a quarter of the egg whites into the yolk mixture, then pour the yolk mixture over the remaining whites, and sprinkle with the flour. Fold the mixtures together until fully blended. Turn into the tin, level with a spatula, and bake at 180°C, 350°F, Gas 4, for 15 minutes, or until lightly browned. Invert on to greaseproof paper, cool and peel off the backing sheet.

For the filling, beat the cheese until soft with the sugar and cream. Divide into two equal portions. Chop the fruit, grate the chocolate if used, and fold both into 1 portion.

Line the base of a 20×10×7cm (8×4×3 inch) loaf tin. Cut a piece of the cake to fit the base of the tin. Cover it evenly with the plain cheese mixture. Cut a second piece of the cake and fit into the loaf tin. Spoon over it the cheese and fruit mixture. Level the top. Trim the remaining cake to fit the top of the tin. Lay it on the mixture, and cover with greaseproof paper. Place a light weight on top, and chill overnight.

Whip the cream for the covering, adding the icing sugar while whipping. Remove the cheesecake from the tin by inverting it on to a serving plate. Cover it smoothly with most of the cream, using a palette knife or spatula for spreading. Pipe the remaining cream in whorls or rosettes. Chop the fruit and use to decorate the cheesecake if desired.

Variation
Liqueured Party Cheesecake
Make as above but add 4 tablespoons Grand Marnier to the cheese mixture without fruit, and 4 tablespoons of the same liqueur to the whipped cream covering.

Cassata Cheesecake

APRICOT JAM CHEESECAKE

Serves 8

BASE
60g (2oz) butter
175g (6oz) shortbread biscuit crumbs
grated rind 1 orange
40g (1½oz) castor sugar

FILLING
300ml (½ pint) water
1½ packets (25g/¾oz) gelatine
juice 1 orange
6 tablespoons smooth apricot jam
500g (1 lb) low-fat soft cheese
5 tablespoons whipping cream

TOPPING
canned apricot halves **or** apricot jam to decorate

Using bakewell paper, line and grease the base of a 20cm (8 inch) loose-based cake tin. Do not fit the sides on to the base for the moment. Soften the butter and work in the crumbs, 1 teaspoon orange rind and sugar. Press the mixture all over the base of the tin, leaving the edge clear. Put on a baking sheet and bake for 8 minutes at 180°C, 350°F, Gas 4. Cool. Fit the sides on the tin.

Put the water in a small heatproof bowl. Sprinkle on the gelatine and allow to soften. Stand the container in a pan of very hot water, and stir until the gelatine dissolves. Add the remaining orange rind, and strain and add the orange juice. Cool or chill until quite cold but not yet set.

Spread 2 tablespoons jam over the cooled baked base, then beat the rest into the cheese until blended. Beat in the gelatine mixture gradually, taking care not to let lumps of jelly form. Whip the cream and fold in evenly. Turn the mixture on to the prepared base, and chill until set. Remove the cheesecake from the tin. Before serving place a ring of canned apricot halves (well-drained), or spoon a ring of apricot jam round the edge of the cheesecake.

SPECIAL QUARK CHEESECAKE

Serves 4–6

BASE
90g (3oz) digestive biscuit **or**
gingernut crumbs
30g (1oz) butter

FILLING
1 egg, separated
grated rind and juice 1 lemon
2 tablespoons milk
40g (1½oz)+½ tablespoon castor sugar
2 tablespoons cold water
1 tablespoon gelatine
150ml (¼pint) double cream
250g (8oz) quark cheese

TOPPING
fresh **or** canned fruit
whipped cream to decorate

Line and grease the inside of a 15cm (6 inch) loose-based or springform cake tin. Make sure the crumbs are fine and even. Melt the butter, stir in the crumbs, and press evenly all over the base of the tin. Bake at 200°C, 400°F, Gas 6, for 5–8 minutes, until lightly browned. Cool while making the filling.

In the top of a double boiler, mix together the egg yolk, lemon rind, milk and 40g (1½ oz) sugar. Stir over simmering water in the boiler until the custard thickens slightly (about 4 minutes). Remove from the heat. Put the water in a small heatproof bowl. Sprinkle on the gelatine and allow to soften. Then stand the bowl in very hot water and stir until the gelatine dissolves. Stir the mixture into the custard, add the lemon juice and leave to cool. While cooling, whisk the egg white with the remaining sugar until fairly stiff, and, separately, whip the cream until it holds soft peaks.

When the custard mixture has almost cooled, blend a little of it with the quark cheese to loosen it, then mix in the rest smoothly. Fold in the egg white, then the cream. Turn on to the baked, cooled base and chill for 4–6 hours, or overnight, until set. Remove from the tin, and decorate with fruit and rosettes of whipped cream.

ALMOND AND SHERRY CHEESE TORTE

Serves 6

12 boudoir **or** sponge finger biscuits
2½ tablespoons cold water
4 teaspoons gelatine
2 egg whites
250g (8oz) low-fat soft cheese
100g (3½oz) castor sugar
150ml (¼ pint) double cream
6 drops almond essence **or** to taste
5 tablespoons sweet sherry
toasted flaked almonds (optional, see page 17)

Crush 4 biscuits to fine even crumbs. Cut the ends off the rest so that they fit in a radiating or star pattern in an 18cm (7 inch) cake tin. Keep them aside with the cut ends. Grease the inside of the cake tin generously with butter, and coat with the crumbs. Reserve any crumbs left over. Put the water in a small heatproof bowl, sprinkle on the gelatine and allow to soften. Then stand the bowl in a pan of very hot water and stir until the gelatine dissolves. Cool to tepid.

While cooling, beat the egg whites until fairly stiff. In a separate bowl, beat the cheese with the sugar until soft and creamy. Whip the cream until fairly stiff, and blend it into the cheese mixture with the almond essence. Trickle and beat in the dissolved gelatine, taking care not to let lumps of jelly form. Taste and adjust the flavouring if desired. Fold in the egg whites as lightly as possible. Turn half the mixture into the tin and spread evenly. Dip the cut biscuits in the sherry, and arrange in a star pattern on the mixture. Fit in the cut ends between them to cover the surface. Spread the remaining cheese mixture on top. Chill until set. Remove from the tin, and decorate with any reserved crumbs or with the nuts just before serving.

ALMOND AND ORANGE CHEESECAKE

Serves 4–6

BASE
250g (8oz) almond macaroons
90g (3oz) butter
1–2 drops almond essence

FILLING
grated rind and juice 1 orange
1 packet (15g/½oz) gelatine
250g (8oz) low-fat soft cheese
150ml (¼ pint) natural yogurt
2 tablespoons clear honey

TOPPING
1 orange
toasted flaked almonds (see page 17)

Line and lightly grease the inside of a 15cm (6 inch) loose-based sandwich cake tin. Crush the macaroons to fine even crumbs, removing any rice paper. Melt the butter, and stir in the crumbs and essence. Press the crumbs evenly all over the base and sides of the tin. Trim the top, and brush off any loose crumbs as described on page 14. Bake for 10 minutes at 180°C, 350°F, Gas 4. Cool completely.

Put the orange juice in a small heatproof bowl. Sprinkle on the gelatine and allow to soften. Then stand the bowl in a pan of very hot water, stir until the gelatine dissolves, and put aside. Sieve the cheese into a bowl and mix in the yogurt and honey. Stir in the orange rind, and then the orange-gelatine mixture. Turn into the cooled crumb case, and chill for 3 hours or longer before use. Before serving, cut the orange flesh free of all pith, membranes and pips and cut into neat segments. Decorate the top of the cheesecake with the orange segments and nuts, and serve.

FRESH RASPBERRY CHEESECAKE

Serves 8—10

BASE
90g (3 oz) butter
250g (8 oz) sweetened oatcake biscuit crumbs

FILLING
2 tablespoons cold water
1 packet (15g/½ oz) gelatine
grated rind and juice 1 lemon
350g (12 oz) low-fat soft cheese
90g (3 oz) castor sugar
2 eggs, separated
300ml (½ pint) double cream
2 teaspoons kirsch

TOPPING
500g (1 lb) fresh raspberries

Grease the inside of a 23cm (9 inch) loose-based cake tin. Melt the butter, and mix with the crumbs. Press the mixture in an even layer all over the base of the tin. Bake at 180°C, 350°F, Gas 4, for 8 minutes. Cool while making the filling.

Put the water in a small heatproof bowl, sprinkle on the gelatine and allow to soften. Then stand the bowl in a pan of very hot water and stir until the gelatine dissolves. Cool to tepid. Strain the lemon juice and mix the lemon rind and juice into the gelatine mixture.

Beat the cheese with the sugar until soft and creamy. Beat in the egg yolks, one at a time, until the mixture is light and fluffy. Beat the gelatine and lemon mixture into the cheese mixture, taking care not to let lumps of gelatine form. Whip the cream with the kirsch until it just holds soft peaks, and fold into the cheese mixture. Whisk the egg whites until fairly stiff, and fold them in. Turn gently on to the baked base and chill until set.

Hull the raspberries. Remove the cake tin and arrange the fruit on top of the cheesecake just before serving.

GINGER AND YOGURT CHEESECAKE

Serves 8

BASE AND TOPPING
125g (4 oz) gingernut crumbs
30g (1 oz) castor sugar
60g (2 oz) soft tub margarine
60g (2 oz) crystallized ginger

FILLING
200ml (6 fl oz) cold water
2 packets (30g/1 oz) gelatine
250g (8 oz) low-fat soft cheese
125g (4 oz) castor sugar
400ml (¾ pint) natural yogurt
ground ginger
juice 1 lemon
150ml (¼ pint) double cream

Line and grease the inside of a 20cm (8 inch) loose-baked cake tin. Mix the crumbs, sugar and margarine thoroughly. Press in an even layer all over the base of the tin. Chop the ginger finely and scatter 2 tablespoons over the crumb base, putting the rest aside. Chill the base while making the filling.

Put 80ml (3 fl oz) of the water in a heatproof bowl. Sprinkle on the gelatine and allow to soften. Then stand the bowl in a pan of simmering water and stir until the gelatine dissolves. Stir in the remaining cold water and leave to cool.

Using an electric mixer if possible, beat together the cheese and sugar until smooth and soft. Beat in together the yogurt, a good pinch of ground ginger, lemon juice and cream. As soon as the gelatine mixture is cold and slightly viscous, stir it into the yogurt mixture slowly but thoroughly, taking care that no lumps form. Pour the mixture on to the chilled base, and scatter the remaining chopped ginger on top. Chill until completely set. Remove the tin. Serve with ginger and apricot sauce (see page 16) if desired.

Fresh Raspberry Cheesecake

Tangy Jelly Cheesecake

Serves 4

BASE
40g (1½oz) butter
90g (3oz) rolled oats
30g (1oz) light soft brown sugar
1 teaspoon ground cinnamon

FILLING
½ orange jelly tablet to set 300ml (½ pint) liquid
150ml (¼ pint) boiling water
2 tablespoons orange jelly marmalade
250g (8oz) low-fat soft cheese
60g (2oz) castor sugar
grated rind 1 orange

TOPPING
½ orange jelly tablet to set 300ml (½ pint) liquid
juice 1 orange
boiling water as required

Line the base and grease the inside of a 15cm (6 inch) loose-based cake tin. Melt the butter, and stir in the oats, sugar and cinnamon. Mix well adding a little more melted butter if necessary. Press the mixture evenly all over the base of the tin. Chill while making the filling.

Chop the ½ jelly tablet, put in a heatproof bowl and pour the water over. Stir until the jelly has dissolved. Leave to cool for 30 minutes or until almost cold and just beginning to thicken. While cooling, spread the marmalade thinly over the chilled base. Beat the cheese until soft and beat in the sugar and orange rind.

When the jelly is almost at setting point, mix it lightly, a few spoonfuls at a time, into the cheese mixture. Do not let lumps of jelly form. Turn the mixture on to the chilled base, cover loosely and chill again until set.

Make a jelly for the topping in the same way, using the ½ jelly tablet and orange juice made up to 150ml (¼ pint) with boiling water. Stir until the jelly dissolves. Cool. Just before it reaches setting point, pour a few spoonfuls over the chilled cheesecake, leaving any remaining jelly to set. Tilt and rotate the tin to spread it evenly over the surface before it sets. Chill for at least 30 minutes. Chop any remaining jelly and arrange round the edge of the cheesecake. Then remove the tin and serve.

LIME CHEESECAKE

Serves 8

BASE
60g (2oz) gingernut crumbs
60g (2oz) Butter Osborne biscuit crumbs
2 tablespoons castor sugar
60g (2oz) soft tub margarine

FILLING
lime jelly tablet to set 600ml (1 pint) liquid
1 packet (15g/½oz) gelatine
200ml (6 fl oz) undiluted, sweetened lime juice
250g (8oz) low-fat soft cheese
125g (4oz) castor sugar
300ml (½ pint) natural yogurt
1×410g (14½ oz) can unsweetened evaporated milk
4 tablespoons double **or** whipping cream
3–4 drops green food colouring

TOPPING
30g (1oz) angelica

Line the base and grease the inside of a 23cm (9 inch) loose-based or springform cake tin. Mix the crumbs, sugar and margarine thoroughly. Press evenly all over the base of the tin.

Chop the jelly tablet. Add the unflavoured gelatine to the chopped jelly in a small saucepan, and pour the lime juice over. Heat gently, stirring, until the jelly and gelatine dissolve. Cool.

Using an electric mixer if possible, beat together the cheese and sugar for the filling until smooth and soft. Beat in the yogurt, then the evaporated milk and cream. As soon as the jelly mixture is cold and viscous, stir it in slowly and thoroughly, without letting lumps of jelly form. Stir in the food colouring. Pour the mixture on to the chilled base. Chill until set, then remove the tin. Finely chop the angelica and scatter it over the top. Serve with single cream.

EASTER HOLIDAY CHEESE GÂTEAU

Serves 4—6

1 round sponge **or** light fruit cake about 15cm
(6 inches) across and 7.5cm (3 inches) high
2×226g (8oz) cartons cottage cheese
125g (4oz) castor sugar
1 tablespoon double cream
salt, ground cinnamon
2 tablespoons sweet sherry
2 tablespoons lemon juice
60g (2oz) chopped mixed peel
250g (8oz) marzipan
apricot glaze as required (see page 15)
small sugar Easter eggs to decorate (optional)

Make sure the top of the cake is flat and level. Split it horizontally into four equally thick layers. Put the bottom layer into a deep loose-based or springform cake tin into which it fits snugly.

Sieve the cheese into a mixing bowl with the sugar. Add the cream, a pinch each of salt and cinnamon, the sherry and lemon juice, and mix until well blended. Fold in the peel. Spread one third of the mixture evenly over the cake layer in the tin. Cover with a second cake layer, and spread evenly with cheese mixture. Repeat the process, then cover with the top cake layer. Place a circle of greaseproof paper and a light weight on top, and leave in a cool place overnight.

Roll out 125g (4 oz) of the marzipan into a thin strip which will cover the sides of the gâteau. Heat the apricot glaze gently and spread it lightly over the sides of the cake. Wrap the marzipan strip round the gâteau, joining the ends with a little extra glaze. Paint the top of the gâteau with glaze. Roll the remaining marzipan into 11 small balls and attach them, at equal intervals, around the rim with dabs of extra glaze if needed. Decorate the centre of the top of the gâteau with sugar eggs if desired.

Sicilian Cheese Gâteau

Serves 4

1 round sponge cake about 15cm (6 inches) across and
7.5cm (3 inches) high
500g (1 lb) ricotta cheese **or** 2×226g (8oz) cartons
cottage cheese
125g (4oz) castor sugar
1 tablespoon double cream
40g (1½oz) bitter-sweet chocolate (optional)
salt
3 tablespoons Marsala wine
60g (2oz) toasted flaked almonds (see page 17)
175–250g (6–8oz) marzipan, tinted green
apricot glaze as required (see page 15)
white glacé icing flavoured with a few drops almond
essence and lemon juice

Split the cake horizontally into four equally thick layers. Put the
bottom layer in a deep loose-based or springform cake tin into
which it fits snugly.

Sieve the cheese into a mixing bowl with the sugar. Mix in
the cream. Grate the chocolate coarsely if used, and stir most of
it into the cheese with a pinch of salt and the wine; reserve
enough grated chocolate to decorate the top of the gâteau.
Chop the nuts roughly and fold into the mixture. Spread one
third of the mixture evenly over the cake layer in the tin. Cover
with a second cake layer, and spread evenly with cheese mixture. Repeat the process, then cover with the top cake layer.
Place a circle of greaseproof paper and a light weight on top,
leave in a cool place overnight, and then remove from the tin.

Roll out the marzipan into a strip which will cover the sides of
the gâteau. Warm the glaze and spread it lightly over the sides of
the cake. Wrap the marzipan round the gâteau joining the ends
with a little glaze. Cover the top with glacé icing. When almost
firm, decorate with the reserved chocolate, if used.

Strawberry Cottage Cheesecake

Serves 6–8

BASE
75g (2½oz) butter
250g (8oz) digestive biscuit crumbs

FILLING
3 eggs, separated
juice 1 lemon
6 tablespoons cold water
2 packets (30g/1oz) gelatine
175g (6oz) castor sugar
salt
250ml (8fl oz) milk
grated rind 2 lemons
1×226g (8oz) carton cottage cheese
250g (8oz) full-fat soft cheese
150ml (¼pint) double cream

TOPPING
250g (8oz) fresh strawberries
icing sugar

Line and grease the base of a 20cm (8 inch) loose-based cake
tin. Melt the butter, and mix in the crumbs. Press evenly all
over the base of the tin. Chill.

To make the filling, beat the egg yolks until liquid and strain
the lemon juice. Put the water in a small heatproof bowl,
sprinkle on the gelatine and allow to soften. Then add the sugar
and a pinch of salt. In a medium-sized saucepan, heat the
gelatine mixture very gently until the gelatine dissolves and the
sugar melts. Stir in the egg yolks and the milk, and continue
stirring until the mixture is almost on the boil, and the custard
thickens. Remove from the heat, and stir in the lemon juice and
rind. Cool. While cooling, sieve the cottage cheese and beat it
with the soft cheese until creamy. When the gelatine mixture is
tepid, mix it into the cheeses lightly with the cream. Whisk the
egg whites until fairly stiff, and fold them in. Pile the mixture on
the crumb base, and chill until firm. Decorate with the strawberries and sprinkle lightly with icing sugar just before serving.

LONGLEY PINEAPPLE CHEESECAKE

Serves 8

BASE
90g (3oz) digestive biscuit crumbs
1 tablespoon castor sugar
40g (1½oz) butter

FILLING AND TOPPING
2×226g (8oz) cartons cottage cheese
1×219g (7¾oz) can pineapple rings in syrup
1 packet (15g/½oz) gelatine
grated rind and juice 1 lemon
125g (4oz) castor sugar
2 eggs, separated
150ml (¼pint) double cream
sprigs fresh mint

This cheesecake is prepared upside down and inverted just before serving. Oil the base of a 20cm (8 inch) loose-based cake tin. Sieve the cottage cheese. Drain the can of pineapple over a heatproof basin, sprinkle the gelatine into the syrup, and allow to soften. Reserve 1 pineapple ring for topping the cheesecake; cut it into neat segments and put aside. Chop the rest of the fruit very finely and mix with the cheese, lemon rind and juice.

Stand the basin containing the pineapple syrup in a pan of very hot water, and stir until the gelatine dissolves. Blend together the sugar and egg yolks, and add them to the gelatine mixture. Stir over very low heat until the custard is the consistency of pouring cream. Cool. While cooling, whip the cream and whisk the egg whites until stiff but not dry. When the custard is thick but not yet set, blend it into the cheese mixture, then fold in the egg whites and cream. Turn the mixture into the prepared tin, and leave to set.

See that the crumbs for the base are fine and even. Combine them with the sugar, then melt and work in the butter to make a crumbly mixture. Sprinkle the mixture over the set cheesecake, and press down lightly. Leave to firm up. Run a sharp-pointed knife round the edge of the crust, and invert the cheesecake on to a 25cm (10 inch) serving plate. Remove the tin and decorate with the reserved pineapple pieces and with mint sprigs.

BUCKINGHAMSHIRE CHERRY CHEESECAKE

Serves 8

BASE
125g (4oz) butter
200g (7oz) digestive biscuit crumbs

FILLING
1×397g (14oz) can sweetened condensed milk
1×226g (8oz) carton cottage cheese
150ml (¼pint) double cream
4 tablespoons lemon juice

TOPPING
500g (1lb) fresh black cherries
150ml (¼pint) water
30g (1oz) castor sugar
or
1×425g (15oz) can pitted black cherries in syrup
1 tablespoon arrowroot
1 teaspoon gelatine

Oil the inside of a 23cm (9 inch) flan case or pie plate. Melt the butter, remove from the heat, and stir in the crumbs. Press the mixture evenly all over the base and sides of the case or plate. Chill for 1 hour.

Tip the condensed milk into a bowl, sieve in the cheese and beat well. Whip the cream until it just holds soft peaks. Stir the lemon juice into the cheese mixture, then fold in the cream. Turn the mixture into the chilled case and refrigerate overnight.

Stalk and pit fresh cherries if used, and cook with the water and sugar until tender. Drain, reserving the syrup, and cool. Drain canned cherries, reserving the syrup. Blend 2 tablespoons cherry syrup with the arrowroot and gelatine to make a smooth cream. Heat the rest of the syrup to boiling point, and stir in the arrowroot and gelatine mixture. Boil for 1 minute, cover the pan and remove from the heat. Cool. Arrange the cherries on the cheesecake, and spoon the thickened syrup over them. Chill at the lowest temperature in the refrigerator for 1 hour before serving from the dish.

INDIVIDUAL ORANGE CHEESECAKES

Serves 2

BASE

2 digestive biscuits

FILLING

2 heaped tablespoons dried skimmed milk powder
150ml (¼ pint) cold water
1 egg, separated
1 tablespoon castor sugar
3 tablespoons orange juice
1½ tablespoons gelatine
1×113g (4oz) carton cottage cheese
salt

TOPPING

¼ teaspoon ground cinnamon
¼ teaspoon castor sugar

Put the biscuits into 2×7.5cm (3inch) straightsided ramekins. In a small saucepan, mix the skimmed milk powder with enough water to make a smooth paste, then gradually mix in the rest of the water. Beat the egg yolk lightly, then stir it into the milk mixture with the sugar. Heat very gently, stirring all over the base of the pan, until the custard thickens. Cover, and leave aside to cool to tepid.

Put the orange juice in a small heatproof bowl, sprinkle on the gelatine and allow to soften. Then stand the bowl in a pan of very hot water and stir until the gelatine dissolves. Cool to tepid. Sieve the cheese into the cooled custard, mix in until fully blended, then gradually trickle in the gelatine mixture, stirring well to prevent lumps forming. Whisk the egg white with a pinch of salt until stiff but not dry, and fold into the cheese custard. Spoon half the mixture gently into each ramekin and leave to set. Before serving, mix the cinnamon and sugar and sprinkle over the top of the mixture.

Variation
Orange and Chocolate Cheesecakes
Make as above but use chocolate digestive biscuits (chocolate side up), and sprinkle with grated chocolate instead of cinnamon and sugar.

SOFT LEMON CHEESECAKE

Serves 6

BASE

1×19cm (7½ inch) pastry shell, baked blind, (see page 12)

FILLING

3×85g (3oz) packets Philadelphia soft cheese
100ml (4floz) lemon juice, fresh **or** bottled
3 eggs
125g (4oz) castor sugar
½ teaspoon vanilla essence

TOPPING

2 teaspoons grated lemon rind

Use the pastry of your choice. The pastry shell should be well cooled if newly baked.

Bring the cheese up to room temperature and strain the lemon juice. Mash the cheese well with a fork. Beat the eggs in a heatproof basin until thick and fluffy, gradually adding the sugar, lemon juice and vanilla essence. Place the basin over a pan of simmering water. Stirring constantly, cook until the custard is very thick; do not let clots form. Beat the cheese into the hot custard, blending thoroughly until smooth. Let the mixture cool completely. Spoon into the pastry shell, and chill well before use. Sprinkle with freshly grated lemon rind just before serving.

Variations
Soft Lemon and Apple Cheese Flan
Use 80ml (3 fl oz) bottled apple juice and 2 tablespoons strained lemon juice instead of lemon juice only. Make as above.

Soft Orange Cheese Flan
Use 80ml (3 fl oz) strained orange juice and 2 tablespoons strained lemon juice instead of lemon juice only. Use freshly grated orange and lemon rind, mixed, to decorate.

TRADITIONAL PASHKA

Makes about 1kg (2 lb)

600g (1¼ lb) dry, home-made milk curd cheese (see page 9) **or** use dry, low-fat soft cheese without preservatives
3 eggs, separated
250g (8oz) sugar
½ teaspoon vanilla essence
150ml (¼ pint) soured cream
125g (4oz) butter
125g (4oz) blanched almonds
2–3 tablespoons chopped mixed peel
40g (1½ oz) seedless raisins

Crumble the cheese and sieve it twice. Separately, beat the egg yolks, adding the sugar gradually, until pale and fluffy. Stir in the vanilla essence and cream. Melt the butter and slowly add to the egg-sugar mixture. Beat until fully blended, then mix lightly but thoroughly with the cheese. Turn into a heavy-based saucepan. Beat the egg whites until stiff, and fold or blend in. Shred the nuts and fold in with the peel and raisins.

Cook very gently in a double boiler, stirring occasionally with a fork, just until bubbles form at the edge of the pan. Cool in the pan.

Use a large flower pot with holes in the bottom, or pierce holes in cottage cheese cartons. Line the pot or cartons with dampened, thin cotton or butter muslin. Fill with the cooled cheese mixture. Tap the pot or cartons once or twice on the table-top while filling to knock out any airholes. Place the pot or cartons on a tray or in a baking tin to drain. After 6–8 hours, lay a circle of greaseproof paper on top of the pot or each carton, and weight it lightly. Leave in a cool place overnight or for 24 hours.

Next day, peel off the paper and turn out the cheese on to a dish, if for use at once, or refrigerate for storage. If left at room temperature, keep covered with a napkin or handkerchief wrung out in cold water.

MODERN PASHKA

Makes about 1kg (2 lb)

500g (1 lb) full-fat soft cheese
250g (8oz) butter
250g (8oz) castor sugar
4 egg yolks
vanilla essence to taste
500g (1 lb) mixed dried and glacé fruits and nuts (sultanas, glacé pineapple, glacé cherries, angelica, flaked almonds)

Sieve the cheese and soften the butter. In a warmed bowl, cream the butter, sugar and egg yolks together until the sugar dissolves and all three ingredients are well blended. Add vanilla essence to taste, then blend in the cheese. Wash and dry any glacé fruit thoroughly, and chop it. Then fold the dried and glacé fruit and nuts into the cheese mixture. Line a pot or cartons as in the previous recipe, and fill with the cheese. Weight, drain, and use or store like Traditional Pashka.

Note When making either traditional or modern pashka use a 1kg (2 lb) weight for a large pot of cheese, a 175g (6 oz) weight for a carton.

APPLE AND WALNUT CHEESECAKE

Serves 8–10

BASE
125g (4oz) gingernut crumbs
30g (1oz) light soft brown sugar
60g (2oz) soft tub margarine
30g (1oz) finely chopped walnuts

FILLING
lemon jelly tablet to set 600ml (1 pint) liquid
1 packet (15g/½oz) gelatine
200ml (6 floz) boiling water
1×410g (14½oz) can unsweetened evaporated milk
1×225g (8oz) packet Philadelphia soft cheese
125g (4oz) castor sugar
400ml (¾ pint) sweetened, smooth apple sauce,
home-made **or** canned
1 teaspoon vanilla essence
1 teaspoon lemon juice

TOPPING
walnut halves
30g (1oz) finely chopped walnuts

Start making the filling before the base. Chop the jelly tablet. Add the unflavoured gelatine to the chopped jelly and pour the boiling water over both. Stir until dissolved, then leave to cool. Chill the evaporated milk and bring the cheese up to room temperature.

Meanwhile make the base. Line the base and grease the inside of a 20cm (8 inch) springform cake tin. Mix the crumbs, sugar and margarine thoroughly. Add the nuts for the base and press evenly all over the base and about 2.5cm (1 inch) of the sides of the cake tin. Chill.

Using an electric mixer if possible, beat together the cheese and sugar for the filling until smooth and creamy, gradually adding the apple sauce, vanilla essence and lemon juice. As soon as the gelatine mixture begins to thicken, beat it in. Then beat in the chilled evaporated milk, and continue beating at high speed until the mixture is thick and light. Pour into the chilled case, and decorate with the walnut halves and chopped nuts. Chill for at least 4 hours or overnight before use.

GARIBALDI CHEESECAKE

Serves 10

BASE
90g (3oz) plain chocolate
75g (2½oz) butter
275g (9 oz) digestive biscuit crumbs

FILLING
3×85g (3oz) packets Philadelphia soft cheese
100g (3½oz) castor sugar
1 packet (15g/½oz) gelatine
¼ teaspoon salt
2 eggs, separated
150ml (6 floz) milk
1 teaspoon vanilla essence
250ml (8 floz) whipping cream
30g (1oz) ground almonds
2–3 drops almond essence
2–4 drops green food colouring

Line and grease the base of a 20cm (8 inch) square pan about 5cm (2 inch) deep. Melt the chocolate and butter for the base, mix with the crumbs, and press evenly all over the base of the tin. Chill while making the filling.

Bring the cheese up to room temperature and beat until soft. Mix 60g (2 oz) of sugar, the gelatine and salt in a fairly large saucepan. Beat the egg yolks lightly in the milk, and add to the pan. Mix well, then stir over medium heat until the mixture is just on the boil. Remove from the heat at once. Beat the cheese into the hot mixture little by little. Cool until barely warm.

Beat the egg whites with the vanilla essence until they hold soft peaks. Continue beating, adding the remaining sugar gradually, until the meringue is stiff and glossy. Mix 2 tablespoons into the cheese mixture to loosen it, then fold in the rest, leaving no lumps. Whip the cream separately until it just holds soft peaks and fold it in likewise.

Divide the mixture in half. Stir lightly into one half the almonds, almond essence and enough colouring to tint the mixture green. Spread it evenly on the chilled base. Gently spoon the uncoloured half on top. Chill for at least 6 hours, then cut in slices or bars for serving.

Garibaldi Cheesecake

CHESHIRE AND APPLE CHEESECAKE

Serves 8

BASE
75g (2½oz) butter
250g (8oz) digestive biscuit crumbs
60g (2oz) muscovado sugar

FILLING
grated rind and juice 1 large lemon
1½ packets (25g/¾oz) gelatine
250g (8 oz) Farmhouse English Cheshire cheese (white **or** red)
2 eggs, separated
1½ tablespoons castor sugar
150ml (¼pint) soured cream
150ml (¼pint) double cream

TOPPING
2 red-skinned dessert apples
lemon juice as required **or** apple glaze (see method)

Line and grease the base of a 20–22cm (8–8½ inch) loose-based cake tin. Melt the butter and work in the crumbs. Sieve and work in the sugar. Press the mixture evenly all over the base of the tin. Chill while making the filling.

Put the lemon juice in a small heatproof bowl, and scatter the gelatine on top. Leave to soften. Then stand the bowl in a pan of very hot water and stir until the gelatine dissolves. Leave until tepid.

While cooling, finely grate or crumble the cheese. Then beat the cheese and egg yolks together until fully blended and pasty. Beat in the sugar, soured cream and lemon rind. Separately, whip the double cream until it holds soft peaks. Stir the cooled gelatine slowly into the cheese mixture, taking care not to let lumps of jelly form. Fold in the whipped cream. Whisk the egg whites to the same consistency as the mixture and fold in. Turn the mixture gently on to the chilled base, and leave in a cool place until set. Do not refrigerate. While setting, quarter and core the apples, and cut in thin, neat segments. Dip at once in lemon juice or apple glaze made as below. Drain well. Arrange in a decorative circle round the edge of the cheesecake just before serving.

Apple Glaze
Measure out 150ml (¼ pint) bottled apple juice into a small saucepan. Put 2 level tablespoons arrowroot in a small bowl, and mix to a smooth cream with a little of the apple juice. Bring the remaining apple juice to the boil in the pan. When boiling, remove from the heat and stir in the arrowroot cream. Return to a very low heat and simmer very gently until thick and clear, stirring once or twice slowly, round the sides of the pan only. Leave until tepid before use. Do not reheat.

CHEDDAR AND HONEY CHEESE FLAN

Serves 4–6

BASE
125g (4oz) Rich Tea biscuit crumbs
60g (2oz) butter **or** margarine
2 teaspoons clear honey

FILLING
1 tablespoon sweet sherry
1 teaspoon gelatine
80ml (3floz) double cream
175g (6oz) mild Cheddar cheese
1 teaspoon lemon juice
60g (2oz) clear honey

TOPPING
90g (3oz) full-fat soft cheese
1½ teaspoons clear honey

Grease the inside of an 18cm (7 inch) flan ring set on a flat serving plate. Make sure the crumbs are fine and even. Melt the fat and honey together gently, and stir in the crumbs. Cool slightly, and press firmly all over the base and sides of the prepared flan ring. Trim the top, and brush off any loose crumbs as described on page 14. Chill until firm.

To make the filling, put the sherry in a small, heatproof bowl. Sprinkle on the gelatine and allow to soften. Then stand the bowl in a pan of very hot water and stir until the gelatine dissolves. Cool to tepid. Whip the cream until fairly stiff. Grate the cheese finely, and fold it into the cream little by little, blending lightly but completely. Strain the lemon juice and mix with the honey, then blend with the gelatine and sherry, and stir into the cheese mixture as lightly as possible. Spread the mixture in the chilled case, and chill again until firm.

While chilling, make the topping. Beat the cheese with the honey until very soft and creamy. Just before serving, remove the flan ring, and pipe rosettes of sweetened, soft cheese on top of the cheesecake.

CHEDDAR AND ALMOND CHEESECAKE

Serves 6—8

BASE
30g (1oz) light soft brown sugar
2 teaspoons golden syrup
100g (3½oz) butter
175g (6oz) digestive biscuit crumbs

FILLING AND TOPPING
60g (2oz) flaked almonds
80ml (3 floz) double cream
175g (6oz) Cheddar cheese
1 teaspoon lemon juice
60g (2oz) castor sugar

Put an 18cm (7 inch) flan ring on a baking sheet. Line and grease the inside of the ring. Melt the sugar, syrup and butter and stir in the crumbs. Press the mixture evenly all over the base of the flan ring. Chill while making the filling.

Toast 30g (1 oz) of the nuts (see page 17), chop them and put aside. Whip the cream lightly. Grate the cheese and fold or stir into the cream with the lemon juice and sugar. Sprinkle the chilled base with the remaining, untoasted nuts, then spread the cheese mixture on top. Sprinkle the top with the toasted nuts. Leave in a cool place until firm. Remove the flan ring, and serve.

INDEX OF RECIPES